Bots

Digital Media and Society Series

Nancy Baym, *Personal Connections in the Digital Age*, 2nd edition
Taina Bucher, *Facebook*
Mercedes Bunz and Graham Meikle, *The Internet of Things*
Jean Burgess and Joshua Green, *YouTube*, 2nd edition
Mark Deuze, *Media Work*
Andrew Dubber, *Radio in the Digital Age*
Quinn DuPont, *Cryptocurrencies and Blockchains*
Charles Ess, *Digital Media Ethics*, 3rd edition
Terry Flew, *Regulating Platforms*
Jordan Frith, *Smartphones as Locative Media*
Gerard Goggin, *Apps: From Mobile Phones to Digital Lives*
Alexander Halavais, *Search Engine Society*, 2nd edition
Martin Hand, *Ubiquitous Photography*
Robert Hassan, *The Information Society*
Tim Jordan, *Hacking*
Graeme Kirkpatrick, *Computer Games and the Social Imaginary*
Tama Leaver, Tim Highfield and Crystal Abidin, *Instagram*
Leah A. Lievrouw, *Alternative and Activist New Media*
Rich Ling and Jonathan Donner, *Mobile Communication*
Donald Matheson and Stuart Allan, *Digital War Reporting*
Nick Monaco and Samuel Woolley, *Bots*
Dhiraj Murthy, *Twitter*, 2nd edition
Zizi A. Papacharissi, *A Private Sphere: Democracy in a Digital Age*
Julian Thomas, Rowan Wilken and Ellie Rennie, *Wi-Fi*
Katrin Tiidenberg, Natalie Ann Hendry and Crystal Abidin, *tumblr*
Jill Walker Rettberg, *Blogging*, 2nd edition
Patrik Wikström, *The Music Industry*, 3rd edition

Bots

NICK MONACO AND
SAMUEL WOOLLEY

polity

Copyright © Nick Monaco and Samuel Woolley 2022

The right of Nick Monaco and Samuel Woolley to be identified as Authors of this Work has been asserted in accordance with the UK Copyright, Designs and Patents Act 1988.

First published in 2022 by Polity Press

Polity Press
65 Bridge Street
Cambridge CB2 1UR, UK

Polity Press
101 Station Landing
Suite 300
Medford, MA 02155, USA

All rights reserved. Except for the quotation of short passages for the purpose of criticism and review, no part of this publication may be reproduced, stored in a retrieval system or transmitted, in any form or by any means, electronic, mechanical, photocopying, recording or otherwise, without the prior permission of the publisher.

ISBN-13: 978-1-5095-4358-8 (hardback)
ISBN-13: 978-1-5095-4359-5 (paperback)

A catalogue record for this book is available from the British Library.

Library of Congress Control Number: 2021949069

Typeset in 10.25 on 13pt Scala
by Fakenham Prepress Solutions, Fakenham, Norfolk NR21 8NL
Printed and bound in Great Britain by TJ Books Ltd, Padstow, Cornwall

The publisher has used its best endeavours to ensure that the URLs for external websites referred to in this book are correct and active at the time of going to press. However, the publisher has no responsibility for the websites and can make no guarantee that a site will remain live or that the content is or will remain appropriate.

Every effort has been made to trace all copyright holders, but if any have been overlooked the publisher will be pleased to include any necessary credits in any subsequent reprint or edition.

For further information on Polity, visit our website:
politybooks.com

Contents

	Acknowledgments	vi
	Abbreviations	viii
1	What is a Bot?	1
2	Bots and Social Life	32
3	Bots and Political Life	51
4	Bots and Commerce	83
5	Bots and Artificial Intelligence	97
6	Theorizing the Bot	120
7	Conclusion: The Future of Bots	140
	Notes	153
	References	159
	Index	188

Acknowledgments

At this point, it's hard to believe there was ever a time in my life when I hadn't heard the word "bot." The last decade of research and learning has been a thrilling journey, and I'm grateful for all the wonderful people I've met along the way. In no particular order, I want to express my deepest thanks to Tim Hwang, Marina Gorbis, John Kelly, Vladimir Barash, Camille François, Phil Howard, Clint Watts, Mark Louden, Frieda Ekotto, Helmut Puff, Roman Graf, Ralph Hailey, Rosemarie Hartner, Chou Changjen, Yao Yuwen, and Yauling and Joel for their support, guidance, and encouragement. I'm continually inspired by all the courageous journalists, activists, and researchers I've worked with over the years, especially my colleagues and friends in Taiwan – your work changes lives. A huge thanks to my friends Sam C., Nate, Amanda, Ike, Anj, Sylvia, Quin, Renata, Samantha, Jake, Jackie, Skyler, Trevor, Jane, and Doug for making life so full and always being up for an interminable conversation. My co-author, Sam Woolley, you've been an incredible friend and colleague, and I'm already looking forward to our next project. Lastly and above all, I'm most grateful to my wonderful family – Mom, Dad, Grammy, Mark, Ben, Britnea, Franki, Rocco, Benni, Murphy, Andi, and all the Monacos and Carmacks. Your love has made me who I am. There's no better family on Earth.

Nick

First and foremost, I would like to thank my family for their constant, enthusiastic, support of my work. Without their encouragement, advice, and love I would never be able to do what I do. To Samantha, Pip, Mum, Dad, Oliver, Justin, Daniela, Manuela, Basket, Mathilda, Banjo, Charlie, and the Woolley, Donaldson, Loor, Shorey, Westlund, and Joens families – a sincere thank you for everything. To all of my friends – particularly Nick Monaco – thank you so very much for all of the learning and laughs. You make each day fun and inspiring. I'd also like to thank the members of my research team, the Propaganda Research Lab, collaborators at the Center for Media Engagement, and colleagues at the School of Journalism and Media and Moody School of Communication – all at the University of Texas at Austin. Finally, I'd like to thank the organizations that support my ongoing research, particularly Omidyar Network, the Open Society Foundations, and the Knight Foundation.

Sam

Abbreviations

AI – Artificial Intelligence
ANT – Actor Network Theory
ASA – Automated Social Actors
CUI – Conversational User Interface
GPU – Graphics Processing Unit
GUI – Graphical User Interface
HCI – Human–Computer Interaction
HMC – Human–Machine Communication
IO – Information Operations
IRC – Internet Relay Chat
ML – Machine Learning
MT – Machine Translation
MUD – Multi-user domain, multi-user dungeon
NLP – Natural Language Processing
RES – Robot Exclusion Standard
STS – Science, Technology, and Society studies

I

What is a Bot?

The 2020 United States presidential election was one of the most impassioned in the country's history. President Donald Trump and his Democratic opponent Joe Biden both contended they were fighting for nothing less than the future of American democracy itself. The election brought with it several events rarely seen in the history of American democracy – an election held in the middle of a global pandemic, citizens' storming of the US Capitol, and attempts by a sitting president to overturn the results of a free and fair election. Unprecedented events weren't only taking place offline, however – *social bots*, or computer programs posing as humans on social media sites such as Twitter and Facebook, were beginning to use artificial intelligence (AI) techniques to fly under the radar of security teams at social media platforms and target voters with political messages. One of the leading bot detection experts in the US bluntly admitted,

> Back in 2016, bots used simple strategies that were easy to detect. But today, there are artificial intelligence tools that produce human-like language. We are not able to detect bots that use AI, because we can't distinguish them from human accounts. (Guglielmi, 2020)

But bots were not only carrying out covert, deceptive, activity online in 2020. Working with amplify.ai, the Biden campaign deployed a chatbot to interact with users on Facebook messenger and encourage users to vote. This bot's intent was not to deceive – it would reveal that it was not human if asked – rather it was a means of using AI techniques to try to boost the get-out-the-vote efforts. Amplify.ai's bots helped Biden reach over 240,000 voters in fourteen states in the three weeks leading up to election day (Dhapola, 2021; Disawar & Chang, 2021). Bots' activities in the 2020 election illustrated the dual nature of the technology – whether bots are "bad" or "good" for society depends on how they are designed and used.

Until recently, the word "bot" was fairly obscure, used mostly in arcane discussions in the academy between scholars, and in Silicon Valley meeting rooms full of computer programmers. The year 2020 was, of course, not the first time bots had been deployed to participate hyperactively in online political discussion in the US. The November 2016 presidential election was the one that gave bots a household name, both in the US and around the world. Journalists and researchers documented the underhanded automated tactics that were being used during that contest to promote both candidates. For many, this was the first time that they realized that political discussions online might not have an actual person on the other end – it might be a piece of software feeding us canned lines from a spreadsheet on the other side of the globe. Now, we can't seem to get that idea out of our heads. These days, social media users quickly label any antagonistic arguer on social media a "bot," whether it's a troll, a disinformation agent, or a true bot (an automated account).

But before bots became a notorious byword for social media manipulation in 2016, they were already a central infrastructural part of computer architecture and the internet. Many bots are benign, designed to do the monotonous work that humans do not enjoy and do not do quickly. They carry out routine maintenance tasks. They are the backbone of search engines like Google, Bing, and Yandex. They help maintain services, gather and organize vast amounts of online information, perform analytics, send reminders. They regulate chatrooms and keep them running when users are fast asleep. They power the voice-based interfaces emerging in AI assistants such as Apple's Siri, Amazon's Alexa, or

Microsoft's Cortana. They carry out basic customer service as stand-ins for humans online or on the phone. On the stock market, they make split-second decisions about buying and trading financial securities; they now manage over 60 percent of all investment funds (Kolakowski, 2019). In video games, they run the interactive agents known as non-player characters (NPCs) that converse with human players and advance storylines.

Other bots are malicious. They amplify disinformation and sow discord on social media, lure the lonely onto dating sites, scam unsuspecting victims, and facilitate denial-of-service cyberattacks, crashing websites by overloading them with automated traffic. They generate "deep fakes" – realistic-seeming faces of humans who have never existed, which can serve as a first step to larger fraudulent activity on the web (such as creating fake accounts to use for scams on dating apps). They artificially inflate the popularity of celebrities and politicians, as companies sell thousands of fake online followers for only a few dollars (Confessore et al., 2018).

As obedient agents following their developers' programming, bots' uses and "interests" are as diverse as humans themselves. They can be written in nearly any programming language. They can sleuth from website to website, looking for relevant information on a desired topic or individual. They are active on nearly all modern social media platforms – Facebook, Instagram, Twitter, Reddit, Telegram, YouTube – and keep the wheels turning at other popular sites like Wikipedia. They can interact with other users as official customer service representatives, chat under the guise of a human user, or work silently in the background as digital wallflowers, watching users and websites, silently gathering information, or gaming algorithms for their own purposes.

This book is about bots in all their diversity: what they do, why they're made, who makes them, how they've evolved over time, and where they are heading. Throughout these chapters, we'll draw on research from diverse fields

– including communications, computer science, linguistics, political science, and sociology – to explain the origins and workings of bots. We examine the history and development of bots in the technological and social worlds, drawing on the authors' expertise from a decade of interviews in the field and hands-on research at the highest levels of government, academia, and the private sector.

It's easy to think bots only emerged on the internet in the last few years, or that their activities are limited to spamming Twitter with political hashtags, but nothing could be further from the truth. Bots' history is as long as that of modern computers themselves. They facilitate interpersonal communication, enhance political communication through getting out the vote or supercharging low-resourced activists, degrade political communication through spam and computational propaganda, streamline formulaic legal processes, and form the backbone of modern commerce and financial transactions. They also interact with one another – allowing computers to communicate with each other to keep the modern web running smoothly. Few technologies have influenced our lives as profoundly and as silently as bots. This is their story, and the story of how bots have transformed not only technology, but also society. The ways we think, speak, and interact with each other have all been transformed by bots.

Our hope is that through this book, the reader will gain a thorough understanding how technology and human communication intertwine, shaping politics, social life, and commerce. Throughout these seven chapters, we'll cover all these areas in detail. In this chapter, we give the history of bots and define the different types of bots. In Chapter 2, Bots and Social Life, we explore the role that these computational agents play across global digital society. Chapter 3 explores the various ways that bots have been used for political communications, for both good and bad purposes, focusing especially on the advent of widespread digital campaigning and social media political bots in the last decade. In Chapter 4, we turn to the role of bots in the private sector, detailing commercial uses of automated agents over time in finance, customer service, and marketing. Chapter 5 explores the intersection of bots and artificial intelligence (AI). In Chapter 6, we trace the history of bot theory in academia – drawing on social science, philosophy, art, and computer science – to understand how the conception of bots has evolved over time and to consider bots' future, particularly as it relates to questions in policy, ethics, and research. Finally, we close with thoughts on the future of bots, and key recommendations for researchers, policymakers, and technologists working on bots in the future.

Where Does the Word "Bot" Come From?

"Bot" is a shortened version of the word "robot." While the concept of a self-managing machine that performs tasks has arguably been around for hundreds of years (for example, DaVinci's 1479 mechanical knight), the word "robot" was not coined until 1920. It was originated by Czech playwright and activist Karel Capek in a play called "Rossum's Universal Robots" ("RUR"). In the play, the titular robots are humanlike machine workers who lack a soul, which are produced and sold by the R.U.R. company in order to increase the speed and profitability of manufacturing. Capek called these machines *roboti* at the suggestion of his brother Josef, who adapted the term from the Czech words *robotnik* ("forced worker") and *robota* ("forced labor, compulsory service") (Flatow, 2011; Online Etymology Dictionary, n.d.). *Robota* has cognates in other modern European languages, such as the German *Arbeit* ("work"). Inherent in these roots is the idea of forced servitude, even slavery – a robot is an object that carries out tasks specified by humans. This idea is key to the understanding of *bots* in the online sphere today, where bots are computer programs that carry out a set of instructions defined, ultimately, by a human. There is always a human designer behind a bot.

While "bot" began as a shortened form of "robot," in the era of the modern internet, the connotations of the two terms have diverged. *Bot* is now used mostly to designate software programs, most of which run online and have only a digital presence, while *robots* are commonly conceived of as possessing a physical presence in the form of hardware – of having some form of physical embodiment. *Wired* journalist Andrew Leonard writes that bots are "a software version of a mechanical robot" whose "physical manifestation is no more than the flicker of electric current through a silicon computer chip" (Leonard, 1997, pp. 7–24). Today, social bots' implementation may involve a visual presence, such as a profile on Twitter or Facebook, but the core of their functioning lies in the human-designed code that dictates their behavior.

History of the Bot

Many people think that bots emerged only recently, in the wake of the incredibly rapid uptake of smartphones and social media. In fact, although they emerged into mainstream consciousness relatively recently, bots are nearly as old as computers themselves, with their roots going back to the 1960s. However, it is difficult to trace the history of the bot, because there is no standard, universally accepted definition for what exactly a bot is. Indeed, bot designers themselves often don't agree on this question. We'll begin this history by discussing some of the first autonomous programs, called *daemons*, and with the birth of the world's most famous chatbot in the late 1960s.

Early bots – Daemons and ELIZA

Daemons, or background processes that keep computers running and perform vital tasks, were one of the first forms of autonomous computer programs to emerge. In 1963, MIT Professor Fernando Corbato conceived of daemons as a way to save himself and his students time and effort using their shared computer, the IBM 7094. While it is debatable whether these programs count as bots (it depends on how you define *bot*), their autonomy makes them noteworthy as a precursor to more advanced bots (McKelvey, 2018).

A more recognizable bot emerged only three years later. In 1966, another MIT professor, Joseph Weizenbaum, programmed ELIZA – the world's first (and most famous) chatbot,[1] arguably "the most important chatbot dialog system in the history of the field" (Jurafsky & Martin, 2018, p. 425). ELIZA was a conversational computer program with several "scripts." The most famous of these was the DOCTOR script, under which ELIZA imitated a therapist, conversing with users about their feelings and asking them to talk more about themselves. Using a combination of basic keyword detection, pattern matching,[2] and canned responses, the chatbot would respond to users by asking for further information or by strategically changing the subject (Weizenbaum, 1966). The program was relatively simple – a mere 240 lines of code – but the response it elicited from users was profound. Many first-timers believed they were talking to a human on the other end of the terminal (Leonard, 1997, p. 52). Even after users were told that they were talking to a computer program, many simply refused to believe they weren't talking to a human (Deryugina, 2010). At the first public demonstration of the early internet (the ARPANET) in 1971, people lined up at computer terminals for a chance to talk to ELIZA.

ELIZA captured people's minds and imaginations. When Weizenbaum first tested out ELIZA on his secretary, she famously asked him to leave the room so they could have a more private conversation (Hall, 2019). Weizenbaum, who had originally designed the bot to show how superficial human–computer interactions were, was dismayed by the paradoxical effect.

> I was startled to see how quickly and how very deeply people conversing with DOCTOR became emotionally involved with the computer and how unequivocally they anthropomorphized it, [Weizenbaum wrote years later]. What I had not realized is that extremely short exposures to a relatively simple computer program could induce powerful delusional thinking in quite normal people. (Weizenbaum, 1976, pp. 6–7)

This response was noteworthy enough to be dubbed the "ELIZA effect," the tendency of humans to ascribe emotions or humanity to mechanical or electronic agents with which they interact (Hofstadter, 1995, p. 157).

Bots and the early internet: Infrastructural roles on Usenet

Other early bots did not have the glamor of ELIZA. For most of the 1970s and 1980s, bots largely played mundane but critical *infrastructural* roles in the first online environments. Bots are often cast in this "infrastructural" role,[3] serving as the connective tissue in human–computer interaction (HCI). In these roles, bots often serve as an invisible intermediary between humans and computers that make everyday tasks easier. They do the boring stuff – keeping background processes running or chatrooms open – so we don't have to. They are also used to make sense out of unordered, unmappable, or decentralized networks. As bots move through unmapped networks, taking notes along the way, they build a map (and therefore an understanding) of ever-evolving networks like the internet.

The limited, nascent online environment from the late 1970s onward was home to a number of important embryonic bots, which would form the foundation for modern ones. The early internet was mainly accessible to a limited number of academic institutions and government agencies (Ceruzzi, 2012; Isaacson, 2014, pp. 217–261), and it looked very different: it consisted of a limited number of networked computers, which could only send small amounts of data to one another. There were no graphical user interfaces (GUIs) or flashy images. For the most part, data was text-based, sent across the network for the purposes of communication using protocols – the standards and languages that computers use to exchange information with other computers. Protocols lay at the heart of inter-computer communication, both then and now. For example, a file is sent from one computer to another using a set of pre-defined instructions called the File Transfer Protocol (FTP), which requires that both the sending computer and the receiving computer understand FTP (all computers do, nowadays). Another of the most widespread and well-known protocols on the modern internet is the hypertext transfer protocol (HTTP). HTTP was first developed in 1989 by Tim Berners-Lee, who used it as the basis for developing the World Wide Web. Before HTTP and the World Wide Web became nearly universal in the 1990s, computers used different protocols to communicate with each other online,[4] including Usenet and Internet Relay Chat (IRC). Both of these early online connection forums still exist today, and both played a critical role in incubating bot development. These were early breeding grounds for bot developers and their creations.

Usenet was the first largely available electronic bulletin-board service (often written simply as "BBS"). Developed in 1979 by computer-science graduate students at Duke and the University of North Carolina, Usenet was originally invented as a way for computer hobbyists to discuss Unix, a computer operating system popular among programmers. Users could connect their computers to each other via telephone lines and exchange information in dedicated forums called *"news groups."* Users could also use their own computers to host, an activity known as running a *"news server."* Many users both actively participated in and hosted the decentralized service, incentivizing many of them to think about how the platform worked and how it could be improved.

This environment led to the creation of some of the first online bots: automated programs that helped maintain and moderate Usenet. As Andrew Leonard describes, "Usenet's first proto-bots were maintenance tools necessary to keep Usenet running smoothly. They were cyborg extensions for human administrators" (Leonard, 1997, p. 157). Especially in the beginning days, bots primarily played two roles: one was posting, the other was removing content (or *"canceling,"* as it was often called on Usenet) (Leonard, 1996). Indeed, Usenet's "cancelbots" were arguably the first political bots. Cancelbots were a Usenet feature that enabled users to delete their own posts. If a user decided they wanted to retract something they had posted, they could flag the post with a cancelbot, a simple program that would send a message to all Usenet servers to remove the content. Richard Depew wrote the first Usenet cancelbot, known as ARMM ("Automated Retroactive Minimal Moderation") (Leonard, 1997, p. 161).

Though the cancelbot feature was originally meant to enable posters to delete their own content, with just a little technical savvy it was possible to spoof identities and remove others' posts. This meant that, in effect, a bot could be used to censor other users by deleting their content from the web. Once the secret was out, users and organizations began cancelling other's users' posts. For example, a bot called CancelBunny began deleting mentions of the Church of Scientology on Usenet, claiming they violated copyright. A representative from the Church itself said that it had contacted technologists to "remove the infringing materials from the Net," and a team of digital investigators traced CancelBot back to a Scientologist's Usenet account (Grossman, 1995). The incident drew ire from Usenet enthusiasts and inspired hacktivists like the Cult of the Dead Cow (cDc) to declare an online "war" on the Church, feeling the attempt at automated censorship violated the free speech ethos of Usenet (Swamp

Ratte, 1995). Another malicious cancelbot "attack" from a user in Oklahoma deleted 25,536 messages on Usenet (Woodford, 2005, p. 135). Some modern governments use automation in similar ways, and for similar purposes as these cancelbots and annoybots: using automation to affect the visibility of certain messages and indirectly censor speech online (M. Roberts, 2020; Stukal et al., 2020).

Another prolific account on Usenet, Sedar Argic, posted political screeds on dozens of different news groups with astonishing frequency and volume. These posts cast doubt on Turkey's role in the Armenian Genocide in the early twentieth century, and criticized Armenian users. Usenet enthusiasts still debate today whether the Argic's posts were actually automated or not, but its high-volume posting and apparent canned response to keywords such as "Turkey" in any context (even on posts referring to the food) seem to point toward automation.

Over time, more advanced social Usenet bots began to emerge. One of these was Mark V. Shaney, a bot designed by two Bell Laboratories researchers that made its own posts and conversed with human users. Shaney used Markov Chains, a probabilistic language generation algorithm, which strings together sentences based on what words are most likely to follow the words before it. The name Mark V. Shaney was actually a pun on the term Markov Chain (Leonard, 1997, p. 49). The Markov Chain probabilistic technique is still widely used today in modern natural language processing (NLP) applications (Jurafsky & Martin, 2018, pp. 157–160; Markov, 1913).

Bots proliferate on internet relay chat

Like Usenet, Internet Relay Chat (IRC) was one of the most important early environments for bot development. IRC was a proto-chatroom – a place where users could interact, chat, and share files online. IRC emerged in 1988, nine years after

Usenet first appeared, coded by Finnish computer researcher Jarkko Oikarinen. Oikarinen made the code open-source, enabling anyone with the technical know-how and desire to host an IRC server. Along with the code, Oikarinen also included guidelines for building an *"automaton,"* or an autonomous agent that could help provide services in IRC channels (Leonard, 1997, pp. 62–63).

The arc of bot usage and evolution in IRC is similar to that of Usenet. At first, bots played an infrastructural role; then, tech-savvy users began to entertain themselves by building their own bots for fun and nefarious users began using bots as a disruptive tool; in response, annoyed server runners and white-hat bot-builders in the community built new bots to solve the bot problems (Leonard, 1997; Ohno, 2018).

Just as with Usenet, early bots in IRC channels played an infrastructural role, helping with basic routine maintenance tasks. For instance, the initial design of IRC required at least one human user to be logged into a server (often called a "channel") for it to be available to join. If no users were logged into an IRC server, the server would close and cease to exist. Eventually, "Eggdrop" bots were created to solve this problem. Users deployed these bots to stay logged into IRC servers at all times, keeping channels open even when all other human users were logged out (such as at night, when they were sleeping). Bots were easy to build in the IRC framework, and users thus quickly began designing other new bots with different purposes: bots that would say hello to newcomers in the chat, spellcheck typing, or allow an interface for users to play games like *Jeopardy!* or *HuntTheWumpus* in IRC.

Given the ease of developing bots in IRC and the technical skill of many early users, this environment was the perfect incubator for bot evolution. Good and bad IRC bots proliferated in the years to come. For example, Eggdrop bots became more useful, not only keeping IRC channels open when no human users were logged in but also managing permissions on IRC channels. On the malicious side, hackers and troublemakers, often working in groups, would use *collidebots* and *clonebots* to hijack IRC channels by knocking human users off of them, and *annoybots* began flooding channels with text, making normal conversation impossible (Abu Rajab et al., 2006; Leonard, 1997). In response, other users designed channel-protection bots to protect the IRC channels from annoybots. In IRC, bots were both heroic helpers and hacker villains – digital Lokis that played both roles. This dual nature of bots persists to this day on the modern internet on platforms like Reddit, where both play helpful and contested roles on the platform (Massanari, 2016).

Bots and online gaming on MUD environments

In addition to Usenet and IRC, computer games were also a hotbed of early bot development. From 1979 on, chatbots were relatively popular in online gaming environments known as MUDs ("multi-user domains" or "multi-user dungeons"). MUDs gained their name from the fact that multiple users could log into a website at the same time and play the same game. Unlike console games, MUDs were text-based and entirely without graphics,[5] due to early computers' limited memory and processing power, making them an ideal environment for typed bot interaction. These games often had automated non-player characters (NPCs) that helped move gameplay along, providing players with necessary information and services. MUDs remained popular into the 1990s, and users increasingly programmed and forked their own bots as the genre matured (Abokhodair et al., 2015; Leonard, 1997).

ELIZA, the original chatbot from the 1960s, served as a prototype and inspiration for most MUD chatbots. One of the big 1990s breakthroughs for MUD bots was a chatbot named Julia. Julia was part of an entire family of bots called the Maas-Neotek Family, written by Carnegie Mellon University graduate student Michael "Fuzzy" Mauldin for TinyMUD environments. Julia, a chatbot based on ELIZA's code, inspired MUD-enthusiasts to build on the publicly available code from Maas-Neotek bots, to hack together their own bot variants (Foner, 1993; Julia's Home Page, 1994; Leonard, 1997, pp. 40–42). Bots became legion in TinyMUDs – at one point, a popular TinyMUD that simulated a virtual city, PointMOOt, had a population that was over 50 percent bots (Leonard, 1996) – which was an essential part of the appeal for both players and developers.

Bots and the World Wide Web

As we have seen, early internet environments such as Usenet, IRC, and MUDs were the first wave of bot development, driving bot evolution from the 1970s through the 1990s. The next stage of bot advancement came with the advent of the World Wide Web in 1991.

Crawlers, web-indexing bots

The World Wide Web became widely available in the early 1990s, growing exponentially more complex and difficult to navigate as it gained more and more users. Gradually, people began to realize that there was simply too much information on the web for humans to navigate easily. It was clear to companies and researchers at the forefront of computer research that they needed to develop a tool to help humans make sense of the vast web. Bots came to fill this void, playing a new infrastructural role as an intermediary between humans and the internet itself. Computer programs were developed to move from webpage to webpage and analyze and organize the content ("indexing") so that it was easily searchable. These bots were often called *"crawlers"* or *"spiders,"*[6] since they "crawled" across the web to gather information. Without bots visiting sites on the internet and taking notes on their content, humans simply couldn't know what websites were online. This fact is as true today as it was back then.

The basic logic that drives crawlers is very simple. At their base, websites are text files. These text files are written using hypertext markup language (HTML), a standardized format that is the primary base language of all websites.[7] HTML documents can be accessed with an HTTP call. Users submit an HTTP call every time they type a webpage's URL into a browser and press enter or click on a link on the internet. One of the core features of HTML – the one that enables the World Wide Web to exist as a network of HTML pages – is the ability to embed hypertext, or "links," to outside documents within a webpage. Crawler bots work by accessing a website through an HTTP call, collecting the hyperlinks embedded within the website's HTML code, then visiting those hyperlinks using another HTTP call. This process is repeated over and over again to map and catalogue web content. Along the way, crawler bots can be programmed to download the HTML underneath every website, or process facts about those sites in real time (such as whether it appears to be a news outlet or e-commerce site).

Initially, these bots crawled the web and took notes on all the URLs they visited, assembling this information in a database known as a "Web Directory" – a place users could visit to see what websites existed on the web and what they were about. Quickly, advertisers and investors poured funds into these proto-search engines, realizing how many eyes would see them per day as the internet continued to grow (Leonard, 1996).

Though Google eventually became the dominant search engine for navigating the web, the 1990s saw a host of corporate and individual search engine start-ups, all of which used bots to index the web. The first of these was Matthew Grey's World Wide Web Wanderer in 1993. The next year,

Brian Pinkerton wrote WebCrawler, and Michael Mauldin created Lycos (Latin for "wolf spider"), both of which were even more powerful spiders than the World Wide Web Wanderer. Other search engines, like AltaVista and (later) Google, also employed bots to perfect the art of searching for[8] and organizing information on the web[9] (Indiana University Knowledge Base, 2020; Leonard, 1997, pp. 121–124). The indexable internet – that is, publicly available websites on the World Wide Web that allow themselves to be visited by crawler bots and be listed in search engine results – is known as the *"clear web."*[10]

Spambots and the development of the Robot Exclusion Standard

We have already seen that bots can be used for either good or bad ends, and World Wide Web bots were no different. Originally used as a solution to the problem of organizing and trawling through vast amounts of information on the World Wide Web, bots were quickly adapted for more devious purposes. As the 1990s went on and the World Wide Web (and other online communities like Usenet and IRC) continued to grow, entrepreneurial technologists realized that there was a captive audience on the other end of the terminal. This insight led to the birth of the spambot: online automated tools to promote commercial products and advertisements at scale.

One of the very first spambots was on Usenet. In April 1994, two lawyers, Laurence Canter and Martha Siegel, contracted a programmer to help promote an advert for their law firm's assistance in the US Green Card Lottery. The programmer decided to use automation to reach as many users as possible. His bot – considered the first spambot on the modern internet – posted the ad to 6,000 newsgroups in under ninety minutes. The incident elicited a strongly negative response from the Usenet community and, in response, one user built a cancelbot that removed all of the spambot's posts from targeted newsgroups (Leonard, 1997, pp. 165–167).

Usenet was a precursor to more widespread spambot swarms on the internet at large, especially email (Ohno, 2018). Incidents like the botwars on Usenet news groups and IRC servers had, by the late 1990s, made it all too clear that bots would not be only a positive force on the internet. Negative uses of bots (spreading spam, crashing servers, denying content and services to humans, and posting irrelevant content en masse, just to name a few) could easily cause great harm – perhaps most damagingly, crawling websites to gather private or sensitive information.

To solve the problem of bots crawling sensitive websites, a Dutch engineer named Martijn Koster developed the Robot Exclusion Standard[11] (Koster, 1994, 1996). The Robot Exclusion Standard (RES) is a simple convention that functions as a digital "Do Not Enter" sign. Every active domain on the internet has a "robots.txt" file that explains what content the site allows bots to access. Some sites allow bots to access any part of their domain, others allow access to some (but not all) parts of the website, and still others disallow bot access altogether. Any site's robots.txt file can be found by navigating to the website and adding "/*robots.txt*" to the end of the URL. For instance, you can access Facebook's instructions for crawler bots at *facebook.com/robots.txt*. As you would expect, this file disallows nearly all forms of crawling on Facebook's platform, since this would violate users' privacy, as well as the platform's terms of service.

The late 1990s saw several high-profile examples of controversial bots that followed these standards, while arguably violating their intentions, and others who proudly flouted them. RoverBot, a crawler that was created in 1996, was one of these controversial bots. RoverBot was a crawler that retrieved a set of websites relating to a pre-specified topic and scraped email addresses from them. The company that built RoverBot then sold these lists of email addresses to paying customers, who used them to send out spam advertisements. While RoverBot certainly had its detractors, the firm behind it insisted that it followed rules (such as the RES) while scraping the web.

Other spambots did not even follow the letter of the law. For example, a bot known as ActiveAgent ignored the RES altogether, scraping any website it could find looking for email addresses, regardless of the site's policies on bot access. The anonymous developer behind ActiveAgent had a different business model, though. Rather than selling the email addresses it collected, it sold its source code to aspiring spammers for $100. Buyers could then modify this code for their own purposes, sending out spam emails with whatever message or product they wanted (Leonard, 1997, pp. 140–144). Thanks in part to malicious developers like those behind ActiveAgent, new spamming techniques quickly multiplied as the web grew. Today, spambots and spamming techniques are still evolving and thriving. Estimates vary greatly, but some firms estimate that as much as 84 percent of all email is spam, as of October 2020 (Cisco Talos Intelligence, 2020).

Clearly, the RES is not an absolute means of shutting down crawler bot activity online – it's an honor system that presumes good faith on the part of bot developers, who must actively decide to make each bot honor the convention and encode these values into the bot's programming. Despite these imperfections, the RES has seen success online and, for that reason, it continues to underlie bot governance online to this day. It is an efficient way to let bot designers know when they are violating a site's terms of service and possibly the law.

Social media and the dawn of social bots

Social media supercharged bot evolution in the late 2000s. During this period, the cost of broadband internet declined, connectivity increased, and computing power grew. A growing number of people began to spend more and more time on social media sites, producing their own content. The entire web began to evolve, shifting from a slow, company-driven, rocky experience to a smoother, sleeker, and user-friendly one in which user-generated content took the foreground. This new user-centric version of the internet came to be known as the *"web 2.0"* (O'Reilly, 2005).

The user-friendly and user-centric web 2.0 had its own problems. Just as advertisers had realized in the 1990s that the World Wide Web was a new revolutionary opportunity for marketing (and sometimes spam), in the 2000s governments and activists began to realize that the new incarnation of the web was a powerful place to spread political messages. In this environment, political bots, astroturfing, and computational propaganda quickly proliferated, though it would take decades for the wider public to realize it (Zi et al., 2010). We'll examine these dynamics in greater detail and depth in our chapters on political bots and commercial bots.

In every case, online environments that are welcoming to bot innovations – Usenet, IRC, or MUD-gaming platforms in the late 1980s and early 1990s, or Twitter in the late aughts – have consistently been strong drivers of bot evolution. The design of these environments, called their *platform architecture*, is just as important as their policies on bots. In MUD gaming environments, users could easily access and modify code to build bot characters in the game; in IRC and Usenet, bots were a necessary infrastructural part of interacting with the platform, and users often enjoyed building their own. Similarly, early 2000s virtual worlds like Second Life were designed in such a way that bot development became more accessible for average users (Lugrin et al., 2008). Now, perhaps most significantly for the era of social media, Twitter's infrastructure is *extremely* welcoming to bots (and was even more so in the platform's early days) (Ferrara et al., 2014; Zi et al., 2010). Twitter's Application Programming Interface (API) makes building and connecting bots to the platform easy, and its infrastructure has arguably done more to democratize bot development and drive their evolution than any other platform or website in bot history.

Different Types of Bots

One problem with understanding bots is the term's ambiguity: the word has several distinct (though often overlapping) meanings. This makes it particularly difficult for policymakers trying to write sensible technology legislation. Indeed, in the words of two communications scholars, the "multiple forms of ambiguity are responsible for much of the complexity underlying contemporary bot policy" (Gorwa & Guilbeault, 2018).

People have been trying to define what bots are since the 1990s, and multiple bot "typologies" have been proposed by journalists, researchers, and academic experts seeking to organize and categorize the profusion of different bots. These typologies vary from informal groupings to more formal taxonomies (Gorwa & Guilbeault, 2018; Leonard, 1997; Maus, 2017; Stieglitz et al., 2017), and some limit themselves to specific subtypes of bots, such as news bots or political bots (DiResta et al., 2017; Lokot & Diakopoulos, 2016). However, the rapid pace of bot evolution means that these taxonomies can quickly break or become out-of-date. Nonetheless, these efforts are extremely important and provide us with footholds with which to navigate the nascent and ever-evolving landscape of bots and their uses, capabilities, and characteristics.

Recognizing the rapidly changing landscape in bot and disinformation research, the bot categories we discuss here are the most important ones at the time we are writing this book. These categories have largely remained relevant for understanding and analyzing bot behavior in the past three decades. This is not an exhaustive list, but it is a useful introduction to the field. Armed with these categories, the reader will be able to grasp modern bots' main uses in the political, social, commercial worlds.

APIs – How bots connect to websites and social media

Before diving into the main categories of bots, we'd like to note the importance of Application Programming Interfaces, or "APIs" in driving bot development in the modern era, the tool through which most social media bots connect to do their work. Social bots proliferated dramatically in the early aughts and the 2010s, largely as a result of more widespread connectivity, the declining cost of computing and bandwidth, and the rise of social media. Social bots are not confined to any one particular platform – they can appear on basically any social media platform, including Twitter, Facebook, Instagram, Gab, Reddit, and YouTube; encrypted chat applications like Telegram and LINE; or regular websites more generally (Assenmacher et al., 2020; Boshmaf et al., 2011; Confessore et al., 2018; Dubbin, 2013; Massanari, 2016; Monaco, 2017; Morales, 2020; Read, 2018; S. Woolley et al., 2019). (We will talk more about how social bots are used on each platform in our chapters on social and political bots.) But the technical design of certain platforms makes them more hospitable to bot activity. This has to do with the website's API.

APIs are a sort of platform-behind-the-platform, a place where computer programs can easily gather data and/or interact with users on social media sites. The data that computer programs can gather from APIs, as well as what actions they can perform on the site, are pre-defined by the architects of that API. For example, on Twitter, computer programs can post messages from a Twitter account, follow other users, or retweet other users' posts, among many other things (Zi et al., 2010). Bots that use API access are generally fairly easy to program and can be easily created by people with little technical skill. Many of the bots on social media sites, especially the earliest incarnations, were relatively simple bots that used APIs (Woolley, 2020a).

It is also possible to program bots that interact with users on social media sites without using APIs. These bots typically imitate human users by accessing a website through a browser (such as Google Chrome or Mozilla Firefox) to interact with specific parts of the website. These bots perform the same functions as human users by following a set of programmatic instructions. They can run invisibly on a computer, and for this reason are often referred to as "headless" (a reference that uses a visible browser as a metaphor for a head). Headless bot behavior can be automated using software packages such as Selenium, Puppeteer, and PhantomJS.[12] For example, a skilled developer could use Selenium to write a program that launches Mozilla Firefox, logs into Twitter, and composes a Tweet that uses the top trending hashtag in the US and includes the @-mentions of three other users who recently used the same hashtag. Generally, headless bots and scrapers require a fair amount of technical skill to program, and they are more useful for passive intelligence and data collection than for direct interaction with other users. However, tutorials for programming these bots are freely available online (Mottet, 2019).

Social bots

The first type of bot worth noting, and one of the most widespread on- and offline, is the social bot. In the broadest sense, *social bots*[13] (like the other types of bots we have discussed) are automated computer programs, but this subcategory of bots is specifically designed to interact with humans. For example, ELIZA, the conversational computer program that imitated a psychotherapist, could be considered an early social bot (Weizenbaum, 1966). Recently, though, the term has taken on a very specific meaning in the popular imagination: since social media appeared in the 2000s, the term has increasingly come to mean computer programs that pose as humans on websites and social media, often designed to promote/criticize a specific product, politician, or message.

Social bots can converse with other users on social media, but they can also be used for other purposes. Votebots can skew the results of online polls. As fake followers, social bots can be used to artificially inflate the popularity of celebrities and politicians. They can skew social media trends by promoting or amplifying content, such as commercial products or political messages. Using the same amplification techniques, they can drown out content their designers do not approve of. "Benign" or creative bots promote art or make jokes. In short, social bots are as diverse as humans.

Chatbots

Chatbots are computer programs that are designed to converse with humans through text or speech (with varying degrees of success). The first chatbot was Weizenbaum's ELIZA, designed in the 1960s, and chatbots remained popular in MUDs, Usenet and IRC through the 1990s. Popular modern chatbots include the AI assistant systems such as Amazon Alexa, Google Home, or Apple's Siri and the commercial chatbots often used for online customer service.

Most chatbots work in one of two ways. Some use pattern searching and pre-composed responses to simulate conversation; this is how ELIZA operated. Others use more advanced AI techniques, such as fuzzy logic or the generation of dynamic responses based on a database (or "corpus") of typical responses. The latest chatbots incorporate advanced machine learning techniques to boost dynamic conversational capabilities and approach human-like discourse. In 2020, OpenAI's GPT-3 bot took chatbots' conversational abilities to new heights using vast troves of language data and

AI techniques to mimic different styles of writing (*Economist*, 2020). We'll delve into these techniques more deeply in Chapter 5, Bots and Artificial Intelligence.

Service bots and bureaucrat bots

Automated agents are often used to carry out the same tasks humans do, but much, much faster and more consistently than humans ever could. This ability can be used in the commercial realm to simplify workflows and facilitate information dissemination. For example, newsrooms frequently automate the publishing, posting, and dissemination of new articles on social media sites using news bots (Lewis, Guzman, et al., 2019; Lokot & Diakopoulos, 2016; Thurman et al., 2019). In some cases, news bots are used to write stories, especially formulaic reports that rely on routine data; in 2016, *The Washington Post*'s Heliograf bot composed brief stories on hundreds of election race results (Peiser, 2019; WashPostPR, 2018).

Bots' efficiency and consistency can also be useful for taking care of non-commercial routine tasks. For example, the DoNotPay bot is a service bot that helps users cut red tape, automating the process of contesting parking tickets online in cities around the world (Mannes, 2019). The bot saves users time by automating the rote legal process, making it quicker and easier to contest tickets; it has saved users millions of dollars in fines since it launched (Johnson, 2016).

Crawlers/spiders

As we saw in the previous discussion of 1990s bots, automated agents are also extremely useful for collecting and organizing large bodies of data and information. For example, during the 2014 mayoral race in the Taiwanese city of Taipei, bots enabled data analytics companies to gather real-time data on voter preferences and reactions to candidates' campaign messages (Liu, 2019; Monaco, 2017). These infrastructural, non-social bots, which often operate quietly in the background, passively surfing websites and gathering information, make up the bulk of bot activity online. When several cybersecurity firms recently reported that bot traffic exceeds human traffic on the web (Imperva, 2020; LaFrance, 2017), they did not mean social troll bots intended to sow political chaos on Twitter. As we have seen, there are many types of bots. When reading reports like these, readers must play close attention to the *context* in which the word "bot" is used: in these reports, "bot" mainly meant crawlers and spiders, which "are an infrastructural element of search engines and other features of the modern World Wide Web that do not directly interact with users on a social platform, and are therefore considerably different than automated social media accounts" (Gorwa & Guilbeault, 2018).

Spambots

As we saw above, spambots are computer programs that send out tens of thousands of messages or emails, often intended to draw users into malicious scams or to sell low-profile products. Some spambots function like crawlers, trawling the internet, looking for accessible comments sections to load up with spam or scraping webpages for email addresses to spam with emails. Examples of these crawler-type email scrapers include the ActiveAgent and RoverBot examples discussed in the previous section (Hayati et al., 2009; Leonard, 1997b pp. 140–148). Other spambots target social media sites, overloading users with malicious links or product promotion (Keelan et al., 2010). While spam is normally aimed at making money rather than disseminating political messaging, networks of social spambots can be reappropriated for political messaging with the flip of a switch (Monaco, 2019a; Thomas et al., 2012).

Cyborgs

The "cyborg" bot is a hybrid type of bot that does not fit perfectly into any of the previous categories. Cyborgs are a special form of social bot – automated accounts on social media that can be thought of as "bot-assisted human" or a "human-assisted bot" (Zi et al., 2010). However, the line between fully automated bot and cyborg bot is fuzzy, for it has "never been clear exactly how much automation makes a human user a cyborg, or how much human intervention is needed to make a bot a cyborg" (Gorwa & Guilbeault, 2018).

Since cyborgs are partially controlled by humans, they leave different, less predictable activity signatures than normal, fully automated bots. For this reason, they are often able to slip through social media companies' cybersecurity and bot detection algorithms. In the past few years, they have become increasingly common as a tool for political messaging (Woolley, 2020a, p. 85); for example, during the 2019 US Democratic presidential primary debates, one cyborg called the *YangGang RT bot* retweeted mentions of candidate Andrew Yang (Monaco, 2019b). Another recent form of cyborg political activism and campaigning is the "*Volunteer botnet*" – the willing temporary donation of one's social media account to be used as a bot for political campaigning (Woolley & Monaco, 2020). We'll cover cyborgs in greater depth in our chapter on political bots.

Zombies, or compromised-device bots

A relatively unfamiliar type of bot for the general public is the "zombie" device – any internet-connected device (computer, phone, fridge, smart TV, etc.) that has been hacked and is controlled by a malicious hacker. These "zombie" devices can become nodes in bot networks, sending out billions of spam emails per day or overloading target servers and websites in what is known as a distributed denial of service (DDoS) attack

(Rodríguez-Gómez et al., 2013). Indeed, most DDoS attacks are carried out using botnets of compromised devices. This meaning of the term "bot" became common in the 2000s (Yang et al., 2014).

Lots of bots – botnets

Automated agents often work in concert with one another in *"botnets"* (short for *"bot networks"*) – a network of computer programs that work together to accomplish the same goal. The networked bots' functions need not be identical: often, the bots in a network perform complementary functions (Cresci, 2020). For example, imagine a small network of Twitter bots that promote the hashtag *#TacoTuesday* on Twitter. The network might have 100 bots split evenly into seeders and promoters, with the 50 seeder bots dedicated to sending out pre-composed tweets that include the hashtag #TacoTuesday and the remaining 50 promoter bots used to retweet and like posts from the seeders. None of the 100 bots necessarily need to follow each other in order to be considered a botnet – they only need to be working toward the same goal. This group of 100 bots is therefore a botnet, for they share the common goal of promoting *#TacoTuesday*.

Botnets are not necessarily networks of social bots, like our *#TacoTuesday* botnet. The word botnet is also used to designate a network of compromised devices – the *zombie bots* described above. When a hacker gains administrative access to a computer, it can use that computer to perform any task, often without the owner's knowledge. (Here, we mean "computer" in the broadest sense: any internet-connected device capable of receiving and carrying out instructions.) When a large number of these compromised internet-connected devices are networked together, a single hacker has a surplus of computing power that they can use to do whatever they want: steal the computer owners' private information, exploit the spare computing power to make money by mining cryptocurrencies (cryptojacking), or use them to crash targeted websites via distributed denial-of-service, or DDoS, attacks.

DDoS attacks work by vastly overloading a website, driving so much traffic to it that its infrastructure collapses – imagine 10,000 cars all trying to get off of a one-lane highway exit at once, or a lecture hall of 1,000 students all asking the professor a question at the exact same time. These DDoS attacks have gotten larger and larger, driving larger and larger amounts of traffic to sites via botnets, because there is an enormous and growing pool of devices available for compromise: the rapidly growing *Internet-of-Things* (IoT). *IoT* is a term used to describe internet-connected devices that we may not traditionally think of as computers – DVD players, refrigerators, smart doorbells, laundry machines, TVs, cars, drones, baby monitors, etc. Because these internet-connected mundane household appliances are rarely designed with cybersecurity in mind, they are far too easy to compromise and turn into botnets. For example, in 2016, the Mirai botnet used over 400,000 internet-connected devices to bring down servers at the French web hosting service OVH and the web application company Dyn. The attack disrupted the services of several popular websites, including Amazon, Netflix, the *New York Times*, and Twitter. (Most of the compromised devices were hacked using a list of just 62 default usernames and passwords commonly used on IoT devices (United States Cybersecurity & Infrastructure Security Agency, 2016).)

Misnomers and Misuse

As the previous section illustrated, the term "bot" can have several possible meanings. However, the most common popular notion of the bot – that of the heavily argumentative troll account or inauthentic social media account operated by a human – is technically not necessarily an automated bot at all: these accounts are more correctly called "sock puppet" or "troll" accounts (Gorwa & Guilbeault, 2018). (Note that the meaning of the terms *bot*, *troll*, and *sock puppet* may differ significantly from language to language. For instance, in Polish, many speakers use "bot" and "troll" interchangeably to indicate a manipulative online social media account, whether automated or manually controlled (Gorwa, 2017a).)[14]

We highlight these misuses and ambiguities in order to help the reader clearly understand what the term "bot" may mean when encountered in the wild. In this book, when we use the term bot, we will *always* be referring to a program that is partially or fully automated.

Important bot characteristics

Finally, there are a range of bot characteristics that can be used to describe a bot's behavior or evaluate its intentions (Maus, 2017).

- **Transparency** – does the bot clearly state that it is an automated agent, or does it attempt to hide its automation, playing itself off as human?
- **Degree of automation** – is the bot automated all of the time? Do some of its actions only occur with human intervention? Can a human operate the bot while it is also performing other operations autonomously? (These questions all relate to the relative "cyborg-ness" of the bot.)
- **Coordination with other bots** – does this bot operate as part of a botnet or with other deceptive human users?
- **Interaction and passivity** – does this bot interact with or engage with human users in any way (likes, retweets, shares, conversation, etc.)? Are other users aware that the bot is present in the online environment? Does it silently surveil or collect data on other users or websites?
- **Intent** – what is the goal of this bot's behavior?

- **Politicization** – is this bot engaged in political or social messaging?

Conclusion

We have only briefly touched on the history of technology and the internet here. Any account of internet history is necessarily incomplete; it not only highlights or neglects the importance of individual activists, contributors, developers, policymakers, companies depending on when it is told, but it also changes so rapidly that it is difficult to capture accurately. Websites and platforms come and go. Services like Geocities, Alta Vista, and AskJeeves that were well known and widely used in the 1990s are virtually unknown today among most young internet users. Similarly, the social media platforms that have dominated internet usage since the mid 2000s may disappear. The internet's future landscape may be defined by different services and companies, ones that are inconceivable today. As one technology historian puts it, *"the history of computing [...] can never be written"* (Ceruzzi, 2012, p. ix). In a sense, the history of the internet is always in beta development: a product that is always taking shape, never in its final form.

Yet there are constants in the ever-changing landscape of the internet. One of these constants is the presence of bots. Bots have been a permanent character throughout the internet's brief history, and they will continue to play essential roles – both infrastructural and social – in the future. This book aims to show the ever-increasing importance bots are playing in human life. Bots can be easy to miss or ignore because they often function in the background, or on the peripheries – or in social situations that are designed to pass themselves off as humans – but they are integral to life and the functioning of technical processes online. On the front end, bots play a role across political processes, business transactions, and social media sites. On the back end, bots are a means for machines to communicate with other machines and keep our favorite technologies running smoothly (or to attack them with malicious intent). In each of these domains, some bots incorporate AI techniques, while others are extremely simplistic in their design. We'll explore each of these areas in depth in the chapters to come, and help readers understand the past, present, and future of online bots, and the undeniable influence they have on our lives.

2

Bots and Social Life

The Twitter bot @everyword was built to tweet each word from the Oxford English Dictionary. From 2007 to 2014, the automated account shared one word every thirty minutes, in alphabetical order. It eventually shared a total of 109,157 words. The bot developed a following of over 100,000 Twitter users, who regularly liked, retweeted, and commented on its content. This account, carrying out its mundane little task, garnered attention from major news outlets, with writeups in the *Guardian* (Spencer, 2014), *The Washington Post* (Dewey, 2014), and *The New Yorker* (Dubbin, 2013). Its creator, the poet and programmer Allison Parrish, explained that the endeavor was a response to people's perceptions of Twitter content as "inane," filled with "people just posting about their sandwiches or whatever"(Fernandez, 2017). How would a bot sharing each English word challenge, critique, or concretize these assumptions about Twitter?

For many, @everyword was both a pointless and poignant exercise – simultaneously repetitive and captivating. It captured the mundane nature of information transmission online, while also subtly revealing the nuances of language and the online experience. MIT professor and computational poet Nick Montfort summed up the bot as "the everyday bot for the everyman. Everyone thinks everything about it, heading everyway to everywhere" (Parrish, 2015). The genius of @everyword was its elucidation of the procedural underpinnings of computer programming, the web, and language, while also provoking deeply human interaction and reflection. It remains an outstanding example of a social bot

(which we define as any bot designed to interact directly with human users.)

Social bots interact with average internet users across a wide variety of websites and platforms. You might encounter them in defined roles, such as the automated digital customer service representatives (chatbots) on your bank's website. Or you might encounter bots in a multitude of less-constrained roles on Twitter, as with @everyword. In a piece defining the "bot," Parrish wrote about what she calls the "PUDG model," which defines bots as "procedural, uncreative, data driven, graffiti" (Parrish, 2016). They are *procedural* in that their "content is automatically generated without human intervention, using a set of predetermined rules and procedures"; they are *uncreative* in the sense that they produce "writing that concerns itself with categorizing, remixing, and re-enacting pre-existing textual artifacts" in order to "draw out something new and unexpected in the process"; they are *data-driven* because they can process a great deal of data, much more than earlier examples of procedural writing; and they are *graffiti* because they are artistic "interventions in a public space (to the extent that, e.g., Twitter can be defined as a public space)." Social bots are thus a mash-up of the computational and the social, the rote, and the surprising.

Online, bots are part of life. Even bots built for less obviously communicative or creative tasks work to form part of the incongruous fabric of internet society. This chapter therefore looks at bots and social life – mostly social bots, but also bots operating on the periphery of society, underpinning cyberspace and the diverse array of digital ecosystems that most of the world traverse on a daily basis. It is situated in this book's broader argument that bots are an integral part of our connected lives the world over. With social bots, as with bots in their other forms, it's easy to forget they exist – they can be almost ambient, particularly when operating in routine customer service roles. Really, though, they are widespread in a variety of roles across the web. They are growing in population and in sophistication.

The core question at the heart of this chapter is: how are bots social? How do they enable interaction and sociality, both intentionally and unintentionally? How are people and bots connected? Why do people personify bots, attributing personality and human characteristics to them? In the following sections we describe the role of bots in global society, referring back to the typology of bots presented in Chapter 1 (Gorwa & Guilbeault, 2018). Broadly, we talk about bots and the internet, and more specifically about bots and social media. We discuss the social role of bots in the domains of journalism, the arts, and dating. We conclude with a discussion of how bots' social role is evolving as innovations in AI and machine learning open up new avenues of social bot output that enable both routine and unexpected behaviors.

Bots and Global Society

The "thing" that we think of as the internet is actually a system, made up of hardware (physical components like cables, servers, and parts of computers, such as monitors or motherboards); software (information or sets of instructions that give directions to the apparatus); and all of the information and interactions take place online. Social media is a similar complex construct that

> consists of (a) the information infrastructure and tools used to produce and distribute content that has individual value but reflects shared values; (b) the content that takes the digital form of personal messages, news, ideas, that becomes cultural products; and (c) the people, organizations, and industries that produce and consume both the tools and the content. (Howard & Parks, 2012)

So, a large portion of both the internet writ large and social media is infrastructural – a combination of the physical and organizational components (the hardware and software) that are necessary for these systems to communicate and create a network between machines, between people, and between combinations of the two. In other words, both the internet and social media are *media* – means of facilitating information sharing and the generation of meaning. As Howard and Parks point out, messages are "cultural products," and the systems that spread them are rich with both social and cultural significance.

Bots are similarly dynamic, especially when we consider them in terms of Parrish's (2016) PUDG model. Indeed, some scholars have argued that bots should be considered, and studied as a whole new form of media (Woolley, 2017). In their simplest forms, bots are simply automated software programs tasked with doing work online. But that exceedingly broad definition ignores people's deeply social, often personified perception of bots. Theories about human–bot relationships and about the nature of bots are explored in Chapter 6. In this chapter, we focus on the social component of the "lives" of bots. What is it about bots that makes people personify them?

We believe that most simply, people personify bots that are used for front-end (direct) communication with both people and other software programs. Forward-facing bots like @everyword are often given names and provided with short descriptions, which seem to ascribe individuality to the bots. Bots on social media platforms like Twitter or Reddit are often given profile pictures and programmed with particular modes of speaking, further cementing perceptions that they are somehow unique. The bots' automated responsiveness (some even leverage AI) invite people to interact with bots as if they have some degree of sentience. Of course, they do not, but bots are (arguably) partially human, for bots are built by people, and they carry the values and – to some extent – the personalities of their builders (Woolley et al., 2018). But, while bots act and interact as extensions of their creators' will and desires, Parrish (2016) notes that bots often do unexpected things that their creators did not intend. This is because they operate online in ecosystems populated by all sorts of other forces and individuals – outside influences that can produce unanticipated behaviors. As Gehl and Bakardjieva (2016) point out, the actions of socially oriented bots can have all sorts of benefits – and they can cause corresponding losses – for users online.

Because bots have all these characteristics – because they are imbued with social meaning, because they are humanized, and because the tasks they undertake are immersed in systems of communication and culture – bots can be seen as enacting social force. What does this mean? First, it means that bots are influential. As we will discuss throughout this book (and at length in the chapter on bots and politics), bots are often used, both directly and indirectly, to persuade computational systems and the people that use them to do certain things. Particularly in relation to politics, this seems somehow Machiavellian or nefarious. But most bot influence is in fact routine or programmatic: most bots aren't explicitly built to manipulate public opinion but to transmit information, but sometimes the act of transmitting information introduces change. Of course, just because there are not always nefarious *intentions* behind programmatic bots or apparently routine algorithms does not mean that the *effects* they produce are necessarily positive, or even neutral: As Noble (2018) points out, minority communities often bear the brunt of these oppressive effects.

Second, bots exert social force because they connect to people. Humans perceive bots as part of their digital communities because they are! For example, moderator bots are a well-known part of life on Reddit. They are specifically designed to interact with the social interest communities known as subreddits, where they monitor Redditors' behavior and enforce sub-Reddit norms. Bots are thus crucial parts of online processes of sociality, both on Reddit and on the internet at large; they are important elements within the formation of digital social groups. Bots participate in social life online in other ways as well, producing art, humor, and/or critique. Automated social media bots (like @everyword and many other bots across many digital spaces and platforms) are built to churn out what Parrish would call "procedural graffiti" aimed at generating interaction, introspection, and – sometimes – simple laughs. Take for instance @mothgenerator, a Twitter bot built to randomly generate beautiful pictures – and associated imaginary nomenclatures – of fictional moths. It functions as "a kind of online, Dadaist encyclopedia of moths" (Voon, 2015).

Other types of bots that connect to people in other ways also exert social force, such as bots that are specifically built to mimic or emulate people. Some act as digital personal assistants (like Siri or Cortana). Others simply engage in either written or spoken conversation with other users online. For example, Microsoft's XiaoIce (known as Zo, Rinna, and Ruuh in other regions) leverages AI and machine learning to connect with users across more than forty digital platforms (including Weibo, WeChat, Kik, and GroupMe) in four countries (China, Japan, Indonesia, and the US) – a significant cultural and geographical arena in which to exert social force.[1]

But XiaoIce's ability to cross platforms is unique. Most bots are consigned to operating within one digital space – they work on Facebook *or* Twitter *or* Reddit, rather than across all three in various iterations. Now, let's examine what social bot activity looks like in various spaces across the internet, particularly on different social media platforms.

Social Bots, Social Media

The most obviously social bots are those designed to communicate directly with other users, such as chatbots. As discussed in Chapter 1, chatbots (such as ELIZA) have existed since before the internet went public,[2] but interest in these bots spiked after Alan Turing's (1950) introduction of the "imitation game" – what is now known as the Turing Test, a way of testing a machine's ability to demonstrate actual human-level intelligence. The Turing Test was taken as a challenge by other early computer scientists – a thrown gauntlet. It was the Turing Test that prompted Joseph Weisenbaum (1966) to build ELIZA, which many users perceived as actually intelligent. In fact, however, ELIZA's responses simply used keyword detection to ask pre-programmed questions, and users attributed sentience to her (as they sometimes do with modern Twitter or Reddit bots, as discussed in a previous section of this chapter). ELIZA was not actually intelligent; she simply presented the illusion of human understanding. She did not even come close to passing the Turing Test (Moor, 2003).

Some bots have actually seemed to pass the Turing test. The best example of this is the bot Eugene Goostman (though its intelligence is still contested by many). The chatbot, designed by a team of Russian and Ukrainian computer scientists to emulate a thirteen-year-old boy, has been an early twenty-first-century fixture of the Loebner Prize competition – a contest that bestows awards to teams whose software programs most convincingly exhibit human behavior. You can read more about Eugene and the Loebner competition in Chapter 5, which provides a deep dive on bots' relationship with AI. In a 2014 UK Royal Society competition, Goostman was successful at convincing over 30 percent of judges that "he" was human. Kevin Warnick and Huma Shah (2016), who were involved in planning the event, argued that this result showed that Goostman effectively passed the Turing Test. Critics, however, were quick to argue. Cognitive scientist Stephen Harnad,[3] angry about media stories reporting that Goostman had passed, said to the *Guardian*, "It's nonsense, complete nonsense. We have not passed the Turing test. We are not even close" (Sample & Hern, 2014). According to Harnad and many others, all existing chatbots simply give the illusion of intelligence by leveraging tricks and humor (as ELIZA did) – misdirections that distract from their lack of actual human understanding.

But does a chatbot need to exhibit genuine human intelligence to be social? How do we define "social" in this context? Socio-technical theorists including Bruno Latour (2007) would argue no – that technologies or tools can have social impact and engage in social behaviors even if they do not have sentience or human intelligence. Latour's actor network theory (ANT), discussed in more depth in Chapter 6, suggests that "things" – including objects and ideas – can generate and participate in interaction considered social or relational. So, chatbots like Goostman and ELIZA, while not *actually* intelligent by most definitions, can be useful social tools for persuasion and manipulation.[4] When we talk about "social bots," though, we mean something specific: "automated social actors" that are specifically built to interact with users on social media systems – whether through written conversation or more passive communication mechanisms such as likes or Twitter retweets (Abokhodair et al., 2015).

Social bots make up a significant portion of users on social media platforms. On Twitter, as Veale and Cooke (2018) point out, they undertake a wide variety of creative and more routine tasks. They often have integral communicative or custodial roles, as with the Reddit moderator bots mentioned earlier or with some types of Wikipedia bots. But the role of social bots on social media sites spreads far beyond that of infrastructurally legitimized positions. Social bots on social internet spaces, from social media platforms like Instagram and Tumblr, to web content management portals like Drupal and WordPress, can be leveraged for all sorts of purposes. They can be interactive, built to act as helpers or service agents for people new to a given space – internet versions of Microsoft's much maligned "Clippy"; they can be messenger bots constructed to notify users about platform updates, tell them about the weather, or remind them about friends' birthdays; they can be "just because," for the purposes of commentary, art, or humor; and – notoriously – they can be designed for malign purposes, such as persuasion, spreading misinformation, or sowing division.

One example of an art or commentary bot, Darius Kazemi's @Twoheadlines Twitter bot, would randomly select two headlines from Google News and mash them together, often with head-scratching results, such as "US grocer LeBron James's online delivery deal sends Ocado shares rocketing" (Kazemi, 2018). Another Twitter bot, @NYPDedits (Backspace, 2015) was constructed to tweet anytime an IP address associated with the NYPD made edits to Wikipedia articles – one of many such "Wikiedits" bots aimed at keeping an eye on powerful entities' actions on the crowd-sourced online encyclopedia. LivePerson, an AI-powered chatbot trained on twenty years of messaging data, can be integrated by companies into numerous services and platforms, including "Apple Business Chat, text messaging, Google Rich Business messaging, Line, Facebook Messenger, WhatsApp, and Google AdLingo" (Chi, 2021). LivePerson also boasts a "bot studio" which allows costumers' to build their own bespoke chatbots for even more messaging channels.

As you will learn in the chapter on political bot usage, bots on many social media sites can be built to follow or comment on other users' content, giving it the illusion of popularity. However, on platforms like Instagram or Twitter, the distinction between automated and non-automated accounts can be very blurry (S. Roberts, 2020). A real human user might regularly log on to their account and post photos or comment on others' posts, but it's possible – even common – for influencers and other highly engaged users to pay for services that automate their likes, comments, and posts while they are away from their smartphone or computer.

How can we distinguish human users from pure bot users? Many of the social media bots mentioned earlier in this chapter – including @Twoheadlines, @everyword, and @XiaoIce – are explicitly tagged by their creators as bots, but many social media accounts do not reveal that they are automated. As author David Kushner (2005) once wrote, riffing on Peter Steiner's famous 1993 *New Yorker* cartoon, "on the internet, no one knows you're a bot." Bots are particularly likely to go unidentified on Facebook, which has a real-name policy and strict guidelines regarding bot usage. Across social media, anonymous bot profiles that do not identify themselves as bots are often involved in malicious and predatory digital behavior, such as online spam or phishing. A digital marketer or social media con artist can amplify their efforts to push a product or steal sensitive information by sending out hundreds of thousands of bots to engage with as many users as possible. Their success rate may be proportionately low, but the automated nature of bots means they do not need to invest much time or labor to cast an extremely wide net; because of the sheer scale of some of these bot armies, enough of these bot-generated entreaties are converted into sales, hacks, and successful scams to make the effort worthwhile. These same wide-net tactics are often used by social or political groups hoping to scale their efforts to manipulate public opinion.

Bots, Journalism, and the News

As these bad-faith bots have proliferated, so have social bots of the non-malign variety. Indeed, bots are now practically indispensable to certain professions. Changes in the field of journalism, including new pressures on the industry's financial model, have forced rapid innovation in the journalism software space, and now many journalism bots are indispensable (Lewis, Guzman, et al., 2019). News bots come in all sorts of shapes and sizes and have all sorts of interactions with society (Lokot & Diakopoulos, 2015). The @NYPDedits Wikipedia bot might be considered a version of a news bot because it is constructed to give those that follow it updates on the edits made to a popular knowledge repository by one of the US's largest and most powerful police forces. The bot is designed to 'keep cops honest' and stop them from making spurious or one-sided claims in encyclopedia articles that concern them in some way. In other words, the bot is part of the fourth estate, aimed at keeping tabs on power. Similar social media news bots built by journalists, news entities, and particularly engaged citizens track the US congress members' mentions of guns (M. Keller, 2015), their stances on marijuana legalization (Woolley et al., 2018) and – yes – their edits to Wikipedia (Cox, 2014).

The same reporters that built the bot that monitors Congresspeople's mentions of guns later launched MockingJay, a version of the same bot that is customizable; it allows users to track other keywords. The bot "follow[s] a list of users and retweet[s] them when they mention a certain topic" (Keller). There is even a Twitter bot that sends out a tweet every time someone publicly lists "drugs" or "sex" as the reason for sending money via Venmo (S. Lee, 2018) – a task some see as an invasion of privacy, dubious though the actual criminality of such interactions may be. All of these bots report data-driven stories via a social-media facing conduit (often Twitter, because of its bot-friendly API and its large userbase of journalists). The idea is that the human users following the bots will help keep track of this automated reporting and notice if someone does something suspect. Of course, these bots are not a perfect solution to the problems facing the journalism industry or the relationship between the public and politicians online; some scholars have argued that Wikiedits bots and the like can make politicians less willing to embrace open-source or crowd-sourced communities like Wikipedia (Ford, Dubois, et al., 2016).

News organizations are also experimenting with other forms of social media or chat-oriented bots. In 2016, the *New York Times* built a Slack bot aimed at connecting readers more directly to the newsroom during that year's presidential election (Gayed, 2019). *The Washington Post* built a chatbot that helps people plan for retirement during the COVID-19 pandemic (Singletary & Shin, 2020). Quartz has scaled its previously named "Bot Studio" into a service it now calls the "AI Studio," which is "aimed at helping journalists use machine learning" (Quartz, 2020). In 2019, Quartz constructed a Twitter bot, @IndiaWatchBot, to help Indians keep abreast of information regarding that year's electoral candidates (Keefe et al., 2019).

Of course, journalism bots come with their own host of limitations and problems. Bots cannot yet – and may never be able to – create nuanced content in news and journalism. Even the smartest AI-enabled chatbots have trouble parsing humor or sarcasm. Like ELIZA and those that have followed her, they tend instead to deflect difficult queries through their own apparent flippancy or cheekiness. Bots cannot yet – and may never be able to – replace most reporting, for it is very difficult, if not impossible, to computationally program a "humane" approach to reporting. A journalism or news bot would have a very hard time capturing the intricacies of human suffering, political malfeasance, or cultural criticism. It would also be extremely difficult, if not impossible, for a bot to carry out complex investigative journalism.[5]

Yet financial pressure on the journalism industry has made it nearly impossible to do journalism without bots. It is now much less common to have paid human journalists doing the more repetitive tasks associated with the news, such as generating classified ads or even writing simple articles on the outcome of minor sporting events. Writing such pieces tends to be very systematic, and changes to journalism's profit model means that there are fewer human journalists on the payroll. Even large news entities have less resources – thanks, in part, to their struggles with the shift to digital. Small-town papers and large media outlets alike are closing with alarming regularity. Bots are, simply put, cheaper and easier to use for writing simple forms of news. When bots do the routine tasks of writing formulaic stories or doing administrative tasks, it frees up the remaining human journalists to do investigative or creative work – work that bots cannot do. Bots also cost less to "employ," for they don't require health insurance or engage in interpersonal conflict that takes up human resource departments' time.

Generally, article writing bots have been used to write rote or predictable articles. Bots are reasonably adept, for example, at writing simple articles about sporting matches, which generally recount which player or participant did what and what the scores or results looked like. In 2019, the *Associated Press (AP)* announced it would "grow Major League Soccer coverage with automated stories" by using "technology from Data Skrive and data from Sportradar to produce data-driven text previews of all Major League Soccer games" (*Associated Press*, 2019). Other bots, like the *Los Angeles Times'* Quakebot, have been used to generate stories on the specifics of natural disasters; Quakebot reports the magnitude of a given earthquake, where it was centered, etc. According to the *New York Times*, "Roughly a third of the content published by Bloomberg News uses some form of automated technology" (Peiser, 2019). The same piece details the news-bot work at the organization Patch:

> a nationwide news organization devoted to local news, [where] A.I. provides an assist to its 110 staff reporters and numerous freelancers who cover about 800 communities, especially in their coverage of the weather. In a given week, more than 3,000 posts on Patch – 5 to 10 percent of its output – are machine-generated, said the company's chief executive, Warren St. John. (n.p., Peiser, 2019)

But, while some in the tech and news industries argue that news bots create a more "objective" journalism because they are mathematical or procedural, even the simplest, most fact-driven bot-reported stories cannot be considered objective. Just as the "objective" recommendation algorithms on YouTube or Facebook are built by people and therefore encoded with their values (Gillespie, 2012), so too are bots of all stripes, including journalism bots (Woolley & Guilbeault, 2016). The bots that write journalism pieces are no more "objective" than their creators; they are built to prioritize certain story elements over others, to use particular article "formulas" over others, and to report on various topics over others. As Ananny & Finn (2015) point out, "the semi-autonomous nature of news bots begs the question of how programmers predict when stories will be timely, appropriate, and publicly valuable." So, news bots – like all bots – have the subjectivities and opinions of their creators baked in. This means that while they can be powerful conduits for sharing or withholding information, they are also bound up in larger power structures that surround the transmission of information. It also means that they create new questions regarding issues such as legal liability, particularly in relationship to how bots and algorithms (more broadly) might complicate issues of free speech and libel (Lewis, Sanders, et al., 2019).

In the future, it is likely that bots will continue to play an increasing role in both the production and consumption of journalism and news. As more and more news entities begin to turn tasks once done by reporters or other newsroom employees over to bots and computational systems it is crucial that they consider the human impact of such decisions (Thurman, Lewis, and Kunert, 2019). These organizations must ask whether or not such moves are positive for both news-makers and news-consumers. There are, moreover, financial implications for newsrooms in both cases. With the former, newsrooms must understand that short-term moves to replace human labor with automated labor can over result in unforeseen costs in the long-term. It is easy, for instance, to overlook the intricacy and nuance that people engage in throughout their day-to-day work. Indeed, the use of AI and automation in a variety of fields can have long-term maintenance costs, which can include a need for increased human labor and other outcomes, often not taken into account when they are launched (Spektor et al., 2021).

Bots, Dating, Videogames, and More

In addition to journalism bots or art/comedy bots like @everyword, @mothgenerator, and XiaoIce, social bots play an important role in purely social online life across all kinds of spaces. They are used to plot compatibility and make connections on dating sites. They are a regular, and often irksome, feature in many online videogames. Online gambling fans might find themselves facing near-impossible-to-beat bots deployed to make money illicitly for their creators. How are these bots beneficial to users across these different digital ecosystems, and how are they used to take advantage of users?

One area of social life that is deeply influenced by social bots is online dating websites and apps. Some readers may be familiar with the story of the now infamous website Ashley Madison, which bills itself as a place for people in committed monogamous relationships to seek an affair. In 2016, Avid Life Media, the company behind the website, admitted to using chatbots to lure users into chats with fake women in order to bolster its claim that the site had a high male-to-female ratio. After the company's use of bots for its marketing scheme was exposed (Light, 2016), reports alleged that the actual ratio on the platform was anywhere from five men to every woman to well over ninety men to every woman (Newitz, 2015; Morris, 2016). Bots also affect dating apps, ranging from Tinder to OkCupid, all of which have a problem with fake bot-run profiles (Rivera, 2020). However, not all bots on dating sites are fake profiles aimed at tricking users. In July 2020, the tech site Mashable reported that bots had potential uses in "AI swiping," in which Tinder users let an automated proxy select their potential dates rather than looking through others' profiles and manually choosing who they are interested in. Mashable's report notes, however, that the use of bots in dating invites all sorts of questions of ethics, discrimination, and bias (Iovine, 2020).

Online video games are another platform with lots of bot activity, both negative and positive. Hugely popular games including Secondlife, Minecraft, League of Legends, and Call of Duty have all dealt with various problematic bots (Lee et al., 2016). Bogus automated accounts are used for a variety of reasons: to build stats, to gain points, and even to convert online currency to offline money. Many bots, known as "farm" bots, are built to harvest game resources. Minebot, for example, is a Minecraft bot that users can purchase to "work for [them] while [they] sleep." It's designed to "stockpile resources, farm items and currency" automatically – in other words, to exploit the system in ways that some would call cheating. At its peak, Blizzard's World of Warcraft (WoW) boasted twelve million subscribers, making it one of the most popular online games of all time (Reilly, 2010). But, according to Indiana University Professor Edward Castronova (2007), WoW bots indirectly cost Blizzard as much as twenty million dollars per year due largely to their role in causing annoyed players to leave the game and customer service costs associated with bot-related complaints. Since that 2007 estimate, costs associated with illicit bot use have likely only grown. This is particularly true given the pandemic boost to the video game industry; in 2020, Bloomberg reported that the video game industry had its best year ever, writing, "time and money spent on games – whether on consoles, computers, phones, or tablets – have soared, as have the share prices of gaming companies" (Glassman, 2020).

But games also offer a space for all sorts of useful bots. At a basic level, some gamers refer to any computational opponent as a bot, and these digital enemies (ranging from game bosses to be fought to the computer you play against in digital chess) are obviously integral to many games.[6] On Minecraft, gamers can use and interact with a wide variety of bots. Researchers at Facebook AI, for instance, built and deployed assistant bots on Minecraft that could "complete tasks specified by dialogue, and eventually, to learn from dialogue interactions" (Gray et al., 2019). There are similar bot assistants across multiple other games and platforms. For instance, the platform Overwolf, which specializes in helping developers create video game extensions, offers GOSU.AI, a chatbot assistant to aid user perfomance on games like League of Legends and DOTA 2.

Other online spaces, too, use interactive bots, some of which are built to pass themselves off as human users. In a piece for the popular tech website VentureBeat, the fraud prevention and mobile measurement company Adjust argued that mobile games, like the popular multi-player console or PC-based ones mentioned above, also suffer from "in-app bot fraud," which they say ends up "wrecking business models by siphoning off revenues and ruining the fun for gamers" (Müller, 2019). The mobile games industry generated $61.8 billion dollars in 2018 and brings in significant income globally, and bot fraud could be equally enormous. According to the bot protection and detection firm DataDome (2020), gambling websites are plagued by malicious bots. Some simply mimic real players on online poker sites and automate engagement with online slots; others, known as arbitrage bots (arb bots) "use web scraping attacks to identify and take advantage of betting imbalances amongst different bookmakers to guarantee they don't lose money and potentially win through arbitrage betting" (DataDome).

Conclusion

Social bots still have an incredibly large presence online, but they have developed something of a bad name with the public, in part because of somewhat sensational reporting on their role in manipulating political events around the globe (Bump, 2017). Bots are now being rebranded, referred to with different monikers or (as AI technology and the hype around it have grown) simply as some version of AI. When we study social bots, we must be careful to cast a wide net in searching for actual social bot use. The definition of the "bot" has always been a bit of a fuzzy one, but in the current era of bots as "boogeymen" those building them may attempt to obscure their bottyness via semantics.

Despite the changes in nomenclature, social bots continue to flourish online, just as they always have. Before the 2016 US election and the revelation that political conversation was being shaped by bots (Howard, Woolley, et al., 2018), Silicon Valley went big on chatbots,[7] with all of the so-called "big five" tech companies – Microsoft, Amazon, Facebook, Google, and Apple – investing significantly in bot technology. The most well-known social bot examples from these firms are obviously disembodied chatbot assistants like Apple's Siri or Microsoft's Cortana, but each company has also put resources behind other social bot formats, such as chatbots on messaging platforms. According to Emerj (Walker, 2019), an AI market research firm, the growth in users on messaging services (now well over 1 billion users on platforms like WhatsApp and Telegram) accounts for a good deal of these companies' investments in chatbots. Emerj also points out that our use of smartphones is changing, and as we use more of the audio and visual capabilities of our phones, chatbots will become even more useful shepherds for navigating non-text based platforms. Social bots continue to play a huge (if often unnoticed) role in our day-to-day lives, even if we talk about them by different names.

When it comes to understanding the role of social bots in society, the important thing to remember is that bots' actions reflect human desires and inputs. The role of the person on the other side of the bot is not an insignificant one. People build bots for all sorts of reasons, including to undertake the socially motivated tasks above: writing news articles, playing video games, mimicking dating profiles, and, yes, talking politics. For the most part, these social bots reflect human society and human desires. Their behavior is usually no more unexpected than that of the person who built them. That is not to say that bots don't deviate from the course set out by their creators. As you'll continue to find out in the next chapters, bots are capable of doing things that cannot be described as purely "procedural" – though they may be "data driven." Oftentimes, unexpected bot behavior happens concurrent to coding mistakes or oversights in design. Sometimes, though, bots do things we don't expect because of complex, opaque, interactions with people other than their creators or with other computational systems. When AI and machine learning enter the mix – when a bot is programmed to learn from its environment – all sorts of unexpected things can happen. The next chapter, on bots and political life, makes this clear by addressing the following question: what happens when bots are used to manipulate public opinion?

3
Bots and Political Life

As with commerce, bots have played a crucial role in influencing politics in the past two decades – boosting or curbing voter turnout, amplifying or suppressing political messages, supercharging surveillance and harassment of dissidents, and even shaping our perceptions of political reality. Our political reality is different today due in part to the bot.

In the early 2000s, as social media and user-generated content began changing the face of the web, a breathless optimism about the liberalizing effect of information technology permeated the culture – not only technology companies, but also universities and governments across the Western world. These optimists held up as evidence the ways that social media had empowered activists to organize massive grassroots protests, such as Colombia's 2008 One Million Voices Against FARC or the 2010–2011 pro-democracy Arab Spring protests across the Middle East.

It's easy to see where the hope stemmed from: technology was indeed playing a crucial role in grassroots organization and democracy promotion around the globe. But few were talking about the flipside of this – the ways that technology was being used to thwart protests in Mexico and Syria, or target pro-democracy activists in Azerbaijan, Bahrain, Russia, and Turkey. At the time, only a handful of academics and activists were preaching the dark gospel about the possible pernicious long-term effects of technology on liberal democracy.

One of the most harrowing of these cautionary tales is that of Boris Nemtsov, a pro-democracy politician in Russia. In the early 1990s, shortly after the fall of the Soviet Union and the beginning of President Boris Yeltsin's new, democratic Russia, Nemtsov got involved in politics. Yeltsin noticed the young Nemtsov's political acumen and charisma and appointed him to his cabinet, where he eventually ascended to the role of deputy prime minister. Yeltsin had actively considered Nemtsov as his successor but came to appoint Vladimir Putin to take his place when he resigned in 1999. Putin went on to win the country's 2000 presidential election and hold onto power ever since (White, 2015).

Though Nemtsov was initially optimistic about Putin's presidency, he grew more wary as the president's actions took an authoritarian turn in the first years of his administration (Nemtsov & Bremmer, 2000). Crackdowns on independent media and political rivals portended a less democratic future for Russia and spurred Nemtsov to vehemently oppose Putin's increasingly autocratic rule (White, 2015). Nemtsov was also one of the few opposition politicians to vocally oppose Russia's 2014 annexation of the Ukraine's Crimea province – an action that also drew censure on the world stage as a violation of international law, and inspired sanctions from the US and EU.

Nemtsov's opposition to Putin earned him the usual battery of treatment leveled at political dissidents in modern Russia – political persecution, physical and digital surveillance, leaking of *kompromat* and, at times, physical danger to Nemtsov and those close to him. Late on February 27, 2015, while Nemtsov was walking in downtown Moscow, blocks from the Kremlin, he was shot four times on the Bolshoi Moskvoretsky Bridge. He died immediately. The assassination occurred two days before Nemtsov was to lead a massive protest against Russia's invasion of Ukraine, and also forestalled the release of Nemtsov's report revealing that Russia had deployed its own soldiers in Ukraine – an assertion that the Kremlin had denied (Luhn, 2015).

Though this was the end of Nemtsov's story, it was the beginning of another – a new story of bots used for political manipulation and disinformation. In the hours after Nemtsov's death, the nightshift at a troll factory in St. Petersburg kicked off. Mysterious accounts appeared on Twitter, spreading messages that cast doubt on Russia's involvement in Nemtsov's assassination, often using the same identically worded tweets – and, as Russia-based American journalist Alec Luhn noted, often accusing Ukraine of having carried out the murder. An open-source data scientist from the UK, Lawrence Alexander, noticed this suspicious activity and began collecting tweets related to Nemtsov's death. Alexander analyzed a sample of 2,900 accounts tweeting formulaic messages about Nemtsov and found they had several suspicious characteristics strongly indicating that they were bots. These accounts cast doubt on Kremlin involvement in Nemtsov's death (Alexander, 2015), and many of them were heavily interconnected – a botnet of accounts that displayed low activity, followed each other, lacked time zone information and didn't interact with other users. These accounts were *political bots,* or software programs used to automate social media profiles in order to manipulate public opinion. Luhn and Alexander were among the first international observers to witness algorithms, automation, and human curation being used together to purposefully distribute misleading information over social media networks. In other words, they were the first to see and recognize computational propaganda in action (Woolley & Howard, 2019).

Most of the Nemtsov bots were extremely simplistic in their design – we've gone as far to call them "dumb bots" for their lack of sophistication – but they worked, primarily because at the time, the public knew very little about disinformation (Woolley, 2020a, p. 82). Early 2015 was still the Wild West in the computational propaganda game; most users had no idea that messages could be manufactured or sent through massive botnets on social media. But such disinformation bots were already rampant. One study on Russian Twitter from early 2014 to late 2015 found that over 50 percent of Russian tweets relating to politics were produced by bots (Stukal et al., 2017). Other early studies found that even these unsophisticated bots could acquire social relevance with simple canned messages, without any attempt to imitate humans or build social trust (Aiello et al., 2014). The disproportionate effectiveness of simple bots in this era was neatly summed up by a hacker with a ten-year career working on electoral disinformation campaigns in Latin America: "When I realized that people believe what the internet says more than reality, I discovered that I had the power to make people believe almost anything" (Robertson et al., 2016).

Only weeks after Nemtsov's death, a digital smoking gun emerged. The bots – and the organized group that ran them – were exposed. Months before the killing, Lyudmila Savchuk, a Russian political activist, had secretly infiltrated the Internet Research Agency (IRA), a troll farm that had been contracted by the Russian government to spread digital propaganda. After documenting the agency's activities for months on the sly, Savchuk decided just days after Nemtsov's assassination to leak internal IRA documents to *Moi Roion*, a Russian newspaper. Savchuk claimed that she and the rest of her team at the IRA were tasked with flooding comment sections of Russian news outlets that reported on Nemtsov's death, accusing the opposition party of murdering its own leader (Chen, 2015). One of the documents she provided was an instructional trolling and propaganda handbook for employees. This handbook contained several topics IRA keyboard warriors were instructed to post about on social media, and one of these topics was Nemtsov's death. This section instructs employees to "lead to the conclusion that Nemtsov's murder was not beneficial to official authorities" and to suggest instead that Ukraine or members of Nemtsov's party had motives for carrying out the assassination. The handbook also contained keywords to include in posts (in part to ensure that they would be pushed up by the algorithms) and news articles for employees to cite.

Throughout 2015 and 2016, other former IRA employees leaked more details about the IRA's operations (Filipov, 2017; Volchek & Sinclair, 2015). In late 2018, officially attributed data from Twitter's election integrity archive corroborated the leaks, showing that in the hours after Nemtsov's murder, Russia's IRA was fervently retweeting messages about the Russian government's lack of motive for killing Nemtsov.

Russia's IRA thus cut its teeth on domestic affairs, but the political bots spreading disinformation after Nemtsov's murder were a harrowing harbinger of things to come. They set the stage for more widespread and insidious uses of computational propaganda for political means. Within the year, the IRA's ambitions would prove to be international (Sanovich, 2017) when it set its sights on the United States' 2016 presidential election, engaging in one of the most successful computational propaganda campaigns in modern history, amplifying political divisions and undermining faith in democracy among a fractious and fractured American electorate.

The Russian government was one of the first to deploy bots and computational propaganda for political ends, but many more governments would adapt the strategy of weaponizing information technology to intimidate, silence, and oppress political opposition in the years to come. Reality itself was up for grabs, and governments, political parties, and private actors alike would soon race to get into the game (Pomerantsev, 2014, 2019). Computational propaganda was here to stay.

Today, computational propaganda isn't limited to autocratic regimes spreading disinformation. In democracies around the world, political bots have increasingly come to be viewed as just another a tool in the digital campaigning toolbox (Bradshaw & Howard, 2019). In the past decade, state-sponsored trolling has targeted independent journalists and dissidents in countries with a wide range of different political systems, such as Azerbaijan, Bahrain, Ecuador, India, the Philippines, and Venezuela (Monaco & Nyst, 2018). In 2018, Saudi Arabia followed the pattern Russia had set with Nemtsov, directing government-directed trolling attacks at Saudi journalist Jamal Khashoggi before his assassination by Saudi agents. Shortly after his murder, Saudi bots and trolls moved to shift blame away from the Saudi government, claiming they had nothing to do with the killing (Benner et al., 2018; Office of the Director of National Intelligence, 2021).

Astroturfing, Inauthenticity, and Manual Messaging

One of the primary uses of political bots is to engage in "astroturfing" – using inauthentic social media accounts to carry out campaigns disguised as spontaneous, popular "grassroots" behavior (Ratkiewicz et al., 2011). The core of astroturfing is the inauthentic behavior. These fake grassroots campaigns use fake accounts to obscure their origins. When fake accounts are automated, they are called "bots." Humans can also run fake accounts, of course. In either case, they are considered to be engaging in *Coordinated Inauthentic Behavior (CIB)* (Gleicher, 2018). Many governments have used real humans to astroturf in the past: China used a group of human propagandists called the 50-cent army to spread positive "cheerleading" propaganda online for the government; in Venezuela, the government set up locations called *Puntos Candanga*, where it would train citizens in how most effectively to spread government propaganda and attack opponents online (King et al., 2017; Monaco & Nyst, 2018). While human-driven astroturfing can be just as dangerous as automated activity, in this chapter we focus specifically on the role played by bots in political astroturfing.

Identifying Bots: Actors, Behavior, Content

Political bots have become cheaper and easier to use in the last decade. Open-source code for building bots is now widely available online; in 2016, there were over 4,000 repositories for deploying Twitter bots on Github, a popular code-sharing website (Kollanyi, 2016). By 2018, there were over 18,000 bot code repositories (Assenmacher et al., 2020). Computational propaganda has become democratized: anyone with the will, knowledge, and resources can use bots as megaphones, broadcasting their message to a large-scale audience as fast as a photon can travel through a fiberoptic cable. This is one of the defining challenges of the digital information age. But not all bots are created equal; dumb bots are widely available and cheap, but the dumber the bot, the less convincing their message will be, and the more likely it will be quickly flagged and removed by security teams.

One of the most effective ways to analyze astroturfing, disinformation, and bot campaigns is the "ABC model," which examines the *actors* behind the campaign, the *behavior* they use to hide their origins and spread their message, and the *content* of the messages – their form and themes (François, 2019). Perhaps the most important of these are the actors, who determine the sophistication (and therefore the impact) of political bots' operations. While there are many relatively small actors in the bot disinformation space – individuals, civil society organizations, small PR firms – the most effective and dangerous actors are the most well-resourced, which are usually governments or large corporations.

The social bots deployed to effect a political goal, known as *political bots*, are used for three main purposes: to game algorithms; to enhance messaging, either by amplifying one's own message or censoring those on the other side; and to surveil the online sphere. We'll dig into each of these three uses in this section, noting hallmark examples of each.

The Tactics Used by Political Bots

One of the uses to which political bots are put is gaming algorithms. Algorithms are the invisible DNA of online platforms – the architecture and functionality of the webpages we visit. We never see them, but they control what we see. By exploiting these algorithms, political bots can influence users' perceptions online.

Search engine algorithms are one major bot target. When traffic to certain websites is increased using bots, this pushes the websites up in search rankings, increasing the sites' visibility. This may be used simply to create more advertising revenue for those running the site, or to push disinformation/misinformation sites up in search rankings, drawing in users who do not recognize them as non-credible sources.

Social media news feed and timeline algorithms on sites like Facebook, Instagram, Twitter, and YouTube are also constantly in algorithm-gaming bots' crosshairs. These content visibility algorithms are the result of a massive amount of invisible back-end number-crunching. How recently a post was created, how many views and interactions it has drawn, and whether it mentions items you tend to be interested in, are but a few of the many factors that influence whether you see a post online. These algorithms are proprietary and are kept under extremely tight wraps to keep them from being gamed but, even without access to the underlying source code, clever engineers can deduce how these algorithms work through guesswork and experimentation. This process, known as *reverse engineering*, can enable malicious manipulators to game algorithms and affect the salience and visibility of content on social media, effectively gaining control over what other users see or don't see on these platforms. This type of gaming is most often carried out by political bots, which are either programmed or purchased by the thousands to like, share, or comment on target posts, thus increasing the probability that other human users will see them and share them, possibly even make them go viral. This was one of the many tricks Russia's IRA used in the 2016 election, targeting the American public with divisive and false news stories to increase political polarization (Howard, Ganesh, et al., 2018).

Algorithms can also be gamed for political purposes by follower bots, which are used to artificially increase an account's popularity on social media. Politicians, celebrities, businesses, and aspiring influencers around the world regularly purchase bundles of fake followers to increase their popularity online and lend them a stamp of social credibility (Confessore et al., 2018). A staffer of former Speaker of the US House of Representatives Newt Gingrich alleged that the congressman had purchased fake followers in bulk in 2011 (Cook, 2011a). External academic and industry observers had noticed that Gingrich's Twitter followers had suspicious characteristics, and one firm estimated that over 90 percent of them were fake (Cook, 2011b; Indiana University Center for Complex Networks and Systems Research, 2011). Even in 2020, when everyone was talking about the dangers of political bots, the practice was still widespread. James Soong, a candidate in Taiwan's high-stakes 2020 presidential election, nearly quadrupled his Facebook following over a weekend one month before the vote in December 2020 – a spike that strongly indicates the purchase of a fake following (Monaco et al., 2020).

Political bots are also used to drive political messaging more directly, through either censorship of an undesired message (called "dampening") or amplification of a desirable message (called "megaphoning") – two opposite goals that bot designers achieve using the same methods. By amplifying or drowning out political messages for a particular target audience, bot designers can shape that audience's political perceptions.

Using bots and computational propaganda to amplify certain content online and give political ideas and actors the illusion of popularity and create bandwagon support is known as "manufacturing consensus" (Woolley, 2018). This concept builds on that of Edward Herman and Noam Chomsky's notion of "manufacturing consent," the principle that mass media can serve as "powerful ideological institutions that carry out a system-supportive propaganda function, by reliance on market forces, internalized assumptions, and self-censorship, and without overt coercion" (Herman & Chomsky, 2002). One recent attempt to manufacture consensus happened in the public comments section on the US Federal Communications Commission's (FCC) proposal to do away with "net neutrality." The proposal received nearly 22 million comments, the vast majority of which opposed net neutrality. On closer inspection, most of it was from bots. The accounts and their comments bore several tell-tale signs of bot activity: comments often used formulaic language with only slight variations, hundreds of thousands of comments would be posted at the same second, and many came from hacked or Russian email addresses and used stolen identities (Bergstrom & West, 2020, p. 34). The fraudulent bot accounts manufactured consensus about net neutrality, making it appear that Americans did not support net neutrality. But they did. When posts from Russian bots were filtered out, 99.7 percent of the comments supported net neutrality; offline polls also showed this same overwhelming support (Mozilla, 2017; Singel, 2018).

Political bots use multiple tactics to manufacture consensus. They dampen or megaphone particular content to sow confusion, amplify harassment of political opponents, and attempt to influence voter behavior directly. We'll examine noteworthy examples of each of these tactics below.

Dampening

One form of bot censorship is *dampening*. Pre-digital censorship depended on a strategy of *information scarcity* – making forbidden ideas and documents harder to encounter, obtain, or discuss. Early internet enthusiasts largely thought the online sphere immune to censorship in this form. This position was neatly expressed by internet pioneer John Gilmore, who famously said that the internet "interprets censorship as damage and routes around it" (Elmer-Dewitt, 1993). By the late 2000s, however, the idea of the internet's invulnerability to censorship began to show some holes in the face of political bots, which depended on a new strategy of censorship that exploited the internet's characteristic *information abundance* (Monaco & Nyst, 2018).

As the history of the early crawler bots showed, bots were always a powerful tool to help simplify unnavigable information overload. As people wrapped their heads around the sheer magnitude of the ever-expanding vastness of the digital universe, nefarious actors began to realize that this vastness could easily be turned to their purposes; the very information abundance that seemed to make the internet censorship-proof could be exploited to create new forms of censorship. If bots could help make the web *more* navigable by gathering and summarizing information, they could also make it *less* navigable by incessantly producing and proliferating information. If bots were actively used to inundate and muddy the information ecosystem, they reasoned, people would give up on finding the truth, or even on the idea of truth. As one information scholar puts it, "information glut can hide the truth by denying attention or credibility to events or facts inconvenient to those in power" (Tufekci, 2017, p. 273). There is no consensus in cacophony.

It is precisely this insight that drives the use of political bots as a censorship tool. *Dampening* is the art of amplifying one message to drown out another. Two specific strategies can be used to dampen undesirable messages: *hashtag displacement* and *hashtag hijacking/polluting*. Hashtag displacement is the art of "bumping" another message out of saliency online. Trending topics on social media are rife for targeting, for they depend on algorithms that can be quite easily gamed.

Especially in the early days, trending topics on Twitter were a simple function of the number of tweets mentioning a particular hashtag or keyword. If more tweets contained a particular hashtag, users around the world would be more likely to see it in their trending topics. Since bots can produce superhuman numbers of tweets in seconds, they were used to target protest and organizing hashtags, drowning them out using other hashtags to take over the top spots in the trending topics and thereby making them less visible. Consequently, with enough bots, an actor could control the narrative around any given topic. Instances of dampening occurred all around the world in the 2010s, including China, Mexico, Russia, Syria, Tibet, and Venezuela (Gallagher, 2015; King et al., 2017; Krebs, 2012; Munger et al., 2019; Qtiesh, 2011; Stukal et al., 2020).

Hashtag poisoning

The opposite approach – overusing a hashtag rather than pushing it down the list – is another useful tactic in the political botmaker's arsenal. Hashtag poisoning occurred during the Arab Spring protests, which were famously organized – and suppressed – online. In early 2011, pro-democracy activists in Syria began demonstrating against long-time President Bashar al-Assad's rule – the beginning of a region-wide protest movement known as the Arab Spring. In response, Assad began violently cracking down on dissidents, both in person and online. Pro-democracy activists frequently used the hashtag *#Syria* on social media to organize efforts, keep up on a rapidly changing landscape, and share information, both with one another and with the global public to keep the pressure on Assad. One researcher noticed that this hashtag began to lose its effectiveness as an organizing tool as anonymous accounts began polluting the hashtag with pro-regime tweets or tweets about irrelevant content (such as soccer-match scores or pictures of Syrian landscapes). A set of seven accounts followed this pattern, tweeting every couple of minutes using protest hashtags such as *#Syria*, *#Mar15*, and *#Daraa*. Later, it would emerge that a private Bahraini company, EGHNA Development and Support, was behind pro-Assad bot accounts spamming the hashtags; the company outed itself by listing one of the accounts in the "success stories" portion of its website (Qtiesh, 2011).

Halfway around the world, the same tactics were used in the campaign to free Tibet from Chinese control. In 2012, cybersecurity expert Brian Krebs noted that *#tibet* and *#freetibet* were being flooded by accounts that seemed to be bots; their other tweets spread spam, and most of the accounts had no followers (Krebs, 2012). These hashtag poisoning attacks on social media were an evolution of a more traditional cyber spyware campaign two years earlier, which targeted the Dalai Lama and Tibetans in exile around the world, infecting over 1,295 computers in 103 countries (Markoff, 2009). These malicious campaigns in Tibet and Syria presaged a new era – one in which the information sphere became a new attack surface in cyber warfare.

DDoS attacks

Political bots can also dampen messages using distributed denial of services (DDoS) attacks, which we discussed in Chapter 1. By overloading a website's servers with millions or billions of requests at a time, bots can effectively take a site offline. This strategy has been used time and time again to target websites and services spreading messages that are unfavorable to authoritarian governments.

All kinds of actors have used DDoS attacks for retaliation. In 2010, the hacktivist group Anonymous carried out "Operation Payback" – a massive DDoS campaign waged on PayPal, Mastercard, and Visa's websites after they stopped processing donations to Wikileaks (Streams, 2012). In Ecuador, DDoS attacks took down the websites of three online media outlets, after they published stories revealing that the Italian spyware company Hacking Team had sold hacking tools to authoritarian governments that had abysmal human rights records (Fundamedios, 2015). The Russian government also favored DDoS attacks in their early forays into cyber warfare, striking both independent Russian media outlets at home, and targeting governments abroad in Estonia, Georgia, Lithuania, and Ukraine (Shachtman, 2009; Clayton, 2014; Markoff, 2008; Soldatov & Borogan, 2015, p. 151).

DDoS attacks strike just about every corner of the globe. The only way to prevent these attacks is to ensure that your network can handle far more incoming data than it is ever likely to receive in the normal course of things – an expensive proposition. A paralyzing attack can always be just around the corner if a well-resourced actor decides to target you with heavy computing power. Large website hosting providers like Cloudflare now include DDoS-protection as a service, and companies like Google's digital rights think tank Jigsaw have built free tools like Project Shield to protect at-risk NGOs and media outlets in repressive states around the world (Sawers, 2019). Despite these countermeasures, DDoS attacks will be an ongoing problem in the future, particularly with the easily hackable IoT devices flooding the consumer market around the world, just waiting to be recruited into botnets.

Amplification

Bots are optimal tools for censoring messages through dampening or DDoS attacks; they are equally useful in amplifying certain messages to reach wider audiences. Political bots that use amplification tactics are building on online automated persuasion campaigns run by private-sector actors as part and parcel of their everyday digital public relations (PR) efforts. Businesses often use bots for astroturfing, inflating the popularity of their products online to gain a competitive edge. One of the first documented cases of this was a marketing campaign from the Korean technology firm Samsung. Using paid writers and fake reviews, Samsung used astroturfing to promote its products and attack local competitors in Taiwan – an incident that came to be known as "Writergate" (寫手門). Taiwan's Federal Trade Commission fined Samsung $340,000 USD for the campaign in 2013 (Agencies, 2013; Kung, 2018b).

Beyond astroturfing campaigns, bots can be used for reputation management, often by individuals or groups who have dark histories that they want to whitewash or keep out of the public eye. Religious cults have used bots to paint their disgraced leaders in a positive light. In India, a hyperactive botnet promotes the teachings of jailed guru Rampal Singh. Singh proclaimed himself a "godman" and started an ashram in India the late 1990s. He was jailed in 2014 after multiple charges of murder and contempt of court. Bots promoting Singh on Twitter (many of which average over 1,000 tweets a day) continue to praise his teachings and status (Monaco, 2019b). Though some of these accounts have been removed from Twitter, many remain online.

These tactics are not limited to reputation management in the private sector. Governments are using PR firms to manufacture political consensus. In the early days of state-sponsored astroturfing, governments often set up their own infrastructure and manpower to execute bot messaging campaigns in-house. As time went on, more and more of this work was contracted out to "black PR firms" – companies willing to carry out these governments' dirty work, running disinformation campaigns and attacking opponents for any paying client (Monaco & Nyst, 2018b; Silverman et al., 2020). By contracting outside firms to do this work, governments keep themselves at arm's length from the digital propagandists, leaving room for plausible deniability in the face of accusations or investigations of digital manipulation (Guo, 2021). In many ways, these private companies carrying out governmental social media information operations are simply another kind of lobbyist, one for the digital age (Brogan, 1993; York, 2012).

Harassment

Political bots are also used to amplify state-sponsored trolling around the world. Azerbaijan, Bahrain, China, Ecuador, the Philippines, Russia, and Venezuela are but a few of the countries where activists have suffered state-sponsored online attacks (Monaco, 2019a). Turkey's online sphere was an early hotbed of bot harassment. In 2013, the pro-democracy Gezi Park Protests took off. These protests opposed President Erdogan and his Law and Justice party (AKP), who had been steadily working to erode democracy in the country. Journalists from independent newspapers covering the protests were viciously attacked by bots. Selin Girit, a reporter from *Cumhuriyet*, received dozens of rape threats per minute at the height of the campaign against her, most of which came from bots (Monaco & Nyst, 2018). Months later, in an attempt to repress future dissent preemptively, Turkey assembled the New Turkey Digital Office, a 6,000-member team of digital propagandists to push the party line (Albayrak & Parkinson, 2013). This office used political bots to push pro-AKP topics and sentiments into Turkey's trending topics on Twitter (Bulut & Yörük, 2017). Since 2013, these bots have consistently amplified vitriolic attacks on journalists and dissidents in Turkey, lending an air of public support to attacks that were in reality being carried out by a handful of people (another example of manufacturing consensus). In some cases, these campaigns succeeded in silencing their targets. The Turkish government has also sought to remove speech attacking its policies (though it was happy to use bots itself against its opponents); in 2014 and in several years since, Turkey has made more content removal requests to Twitter than any other country on Earth (*Hürriyet Daily News*, 2014, 2017; SCF, 2020).

Political Bots and Their Uses

Political bots became widely known to the global public in 2016, when it became common knowledge that they were being used to manipulate elections. Two 2016 elections pushed bots into this new notoriety: the United Kingdom's Brexit referendum and the US presidential election. In the UK's Brexit referendum (which eventually passed, with the UK voting to leave the European Union), researchers from the Oxford Internet Institute (OII) found that online conversation about the event had been dominated by non-human voices. A sample of Twitter conversation from June 5 to June 12 found that an extremely small sliver of accounts involved in the Brexit conversation (less than one percent) had produced over 30 percent of the tweets about Brexit (Howard & Kollanyi, 2016). It was painfully clear Twitter was no longer a "free marketplace of ideas": the messages of those who spoke loudest – often those who could afford to amplify their voices through automation – were heard more often and by more people.

The same year, as the US presidential nominees began their campaigns, political bots flooded the US corner of the internet. In the Republican party primaries, "Latino" bots manufactured consent for Donald Trump in the Nevada caucuses (Woolley & Howard, 2016). After the parties nominated their candidates, this activity rose to "an all-time high" (Kollanyi et al., 2016). A study from the University of Southern California found that in one month alone, 400,000 bots accounted for 20 percent of all election-related political discussion on Twitter (Bessi & Ferrara, 2016). Analyses of Twitter conversation about the candidates during the debates showed that while there were bots supporting both the Democratic nominee Hillary Clinton and the Republican nominee Donald Trump, there was substantially more bot support for Trump than Clinton. Pro-Trump bots outnumbered pro-Clinton bots by a margin of 4:1 in September, and reached 5:1 by election day (Kollanyi et al., 2016). Bots weren't merely being loud, they were also reaching social network positions from which their message diffused more widely (Bessi & Ferrara, 2016; Woolley & Guilbeault, 2017).

Although these vast armies of political bots were everywhere online during the election, the humans that pulled their strings of code had many different interests and goals. Domestic political actors deployed bots to support their chosen candidate, but foreign political actors were also in on the game. Russia's Internet Research Agency (IRA), the same Kremlin-contracted office that had sowed doubt about Russia's involvement in Boris Nemtsov's death in 2015, was targeting the US presidential election with an information operation of unprecedented scale and resources (Howard, Ganesh, et al., 2018; Sanger, 2019). The IRA's campaign wasn't always aimed at creating political support for one candidate or the other; confusion was often good enough – getting voters to disengage was a victory in itself. Citizens who threw up their hands, gave up on the idea of finding the truth, lost faith in the system, or chose not to turn out to vote – these were victories for an actor invested in undermining faith in democracy.

Brexit and the US Presidential election were watershed events in bot history – they put political bots on the general public's radar. However, bots had been interfering in domestic elections since long before 2016. Many already knew that bots are a powerful tool for influencing perceptions about electoral candidates; as one digital marketing and manipulation practitioner in Taiwan put it, having access to bots and fake accounts was like "holding an army in your hand" (Kung, 2018a). Mexico was one of the first countries where this realization materialized into actual digital attempts to dominate and warp national political conversations online. In 2012, bots inundated Twitter supporting President Enrique Peña Nieto's re-election bid. After a presidential debate, bots pushed the hashtag #PeñaGanaDebate, asserting that Peña had won the debate. Automated agents supporting the president and drowning out dissent eventually became so common that Mexico coined a new word for them: *Peñabots* (Baker, 2015). The bot support for Peña-Nieto's re-election presaged a larger wave of technological abuse targeting civil society, journalists, and academics in Mexico after Peña-Nieto was re-elected; in Peña-Nieto's second term, spyware campaigns and at-scale online harassment made the country among most hostile environments for journalists (Reguillo & Maloof, 2015; Scott-Railton et al., 2017).

Mexico isn't the only country to tread this path, for digital campaigning rarely ends when elections are over. After a successful election, digital electioneering machines that promoted candidates and smeared opponents are often converted into an official state-sponsored trolling apparatus of the ruling party; since 2012, this has happened in Ecuador, India, Mexico, and the Philippines (Monaco & Nyst, 2018).

The same year Peñabots flooded Mexico's Twittersphere, another government halfway around the world was targeting its own population to influence the outcome of a domestic election. South Korea's highest intelligence office conducted a digital manipulation campaign aimed at promoting its preferred candidate in the country's presidential election. The National Intelligence Service (NIS) ran a systematic online propaganda campaign to support the incumbent party's presidential candidate, Park Geun-Hye, daughter of the former military dictator of South Korea, and smear her opponent, Moon Jae-in. Park won by a relatively narrow margin of 1.1 million votes. After the election, the NIS's operation came to light. President Park claimed to have no prior knowledge or affiliation with the digital campaign, and in 2017, the then-head of NIS, Won Sei-hoon, was convicted and sentenced to seven years in prison for the operation (Sang-Hun, 2017). The NIS's own investigation of the matter reported that 30 "teams were charged with spreading pro-government opinions and suppressing anti-government views, branding [opposition views] as attempts by pro-North Korean forces to disrupt state affairs" (McCurry, 2017). Prosecutors found that the NIS had posted over 1.2 million tweets in this campaign, but academic researchers estimate the true scale could have been as large as seven million messages (F. B. Keller et al., 2020; Sang-Hun, 2013). This remains one of the few cases where a government has been caught red-handed interfering in its own election and the officials responsible have been prosecuted.

It is clear that bots are being used to influence voters' perceptions of political events, candidates, and issues. But, as the next section shows, bots can also be used in attempts to influence election outcomes directly, primarily by suppressing or increasing voter turnout in certain key areas and by surveilling the political opposition.

Influencing voter turnout

Bot amplification does not always aim at political conversion. Often, it aims at finding out who voters plan to support and influencing voter turnout. If voters can't be flipped, convincing them to stay home will work just as well. Bots have been used to depress turnout in elections and referenda around the world. When the country formerly known as Macedonia held a referendum on changing its official name to "North Macedonia," a small number of hyperactive accounts appeared online and called for voters to boycott the referendum, using the hashtag #Бојкотирам (#boycott). A botnet in the eastern Biafra region of Nigeria used a similar tactic to encourage voters to "stay home" during the 2019 Nigerian presidential election (Woolley & Monaco, 2020).

Surveillance

One of the most persistent political uses of bots is digital surveillance. While the term surveillance has largely negative connotations (and rightly so), we use it here neutrally to mean any kind of data gathering. Of course, surveillance is often used for unethical purposes – such as gathering information for use against dissidents in a larger online disinformation and harassment attack, or a way to impose self-policing and self-censorship in repressive regimes. Surveillance is even used for small-potatoes manipulation: it is surveillance that allows political actors to identify voter preferences and encourage them either to turn out to vote or to stay home. However, online surveillance also has some legitimate uses, such as data collection for social scientific studies on social media platforms, or lawful and sanctioned data gathering by businesses on social media platforms. In all of these cases, good, bad, and neutral, bots are the primary tool used to facilitate at-scale surveillance online.

As the following subsections explain, bot-enabled surveillance can be either passive or active. Passive surveillance is usually silent, running in the background without our knowledge, gathering and processing large volumes of data about users and using it to predict our preferences – buying patterns, voting patterns, social associations, and more. Active surveillance, on the other hand, is out in the open; it can be used for purposes of boosting accountability and creating transparency in certain areas (like Wikipedia's @NYPDedits and Twitter's @YourRepsOnGuns bots from Chapter 2), or for more nefarious purposes like doxxing targets.

Passive surveillance – information gathering and analytics

As we saw in our history of bot evolution in Chapter 1, bots' role as swift gatherers and skilled organizers of online information became apparent in the mid 1990s, when they first began to index the web, creating the backbone of the very first search engines. Today, bots have extended these skills to social media sites, gathering and processing information about users for social, political, or commercial purposes.

Bots can gather information from a social media platform either through APIs (digital "doors" that offer legitimate access to selected data on social media sites such as Twitter) or by scraping target websites (which we might compare to climbing in a window rather than going through a door; scraping can give access to more data than developers intended to share).[1] In either case, bots are engaging in a form of surveillance. If this data is being collected without users' knowledge, or if it is collected for internal purposes (as when large companies trace a user's search patterns or demographic data to determine what products to market to them), it is a form of passive surveillance. These bots are digital wallflowers, quietly collecting information on webpages and users.

Perhaps we can think of this as online *intelligence collection*. It is usually a first step in a larger project; the data collected is analyzed or processed after it is collected. This sort of quiet online data collection often occurs during elections, like in the mayoral race for Taiwan's capital city of Taiwan in 2014. QSearch, a data analytics company, used bots to scrape information on Taiwanese Facebook users in this election. Qsearch worked for one of the two main candidates in the race, Ko Wen-je, and used the scraping bots to build detailed voter profiles and gauge citizens' reactions to Ko's speeches, advertisements, and blunders in real time (Monaco, 2017). Ko won the race; Qsearch and an offshoot group (the political consulting company Autopolitic, founded shortly after Ko's win by one of the co-founders of Qsearch) remain active to this day (Liu, 2019). This is just a subset of more pervasive surveillance and data collection techniques infamously used in 2016 by Cambridge Analytica, which scraped social media and other websites to make granular "psychographic" profiles on voters in the US and then target them with strategically tailored messages for Republican candidates Ted Cruz and Donald Trump (Wong, 2019).

Indeed, governments (or government-contracted private companies) regularly gather detailed data on target persons-of-interest (POIs). Scraping bots are a useful tool for this type of intelligence gathering, as more and more data on individuals is becoming publicly available online. In conversation with the authors, a former member of the US Intelligence Community called LinkedIn "the most valuable intelligence platform in the world" for governments. In 2020, leaks revealed that Zhenhua Data, a Chinese company with links to Chinese military and intelligence, had scraped publicly available online information from websites and social media platforms to compile a database of information on 2.4 million people. The news agency that broke the story called Zhenhua's project "a complex global operation using artificial intelligence to trawl publicly available data to create intricate profiles of individuals and organisations, potentially probing for compromise opportunities" (Probyn & Doran, 2020) – an enormous undertaking that could not have been completed without crawler bots. In the US, a start-up known as Clearview AI used bots to scrape images from Facebook, YouTube, Venmo, and millions of other websites, compiling a database of over three billion images of faces; they used these images to train facial recognition software, which they sold to government agencies and private companies (Hill, 2020; Mac et al., 2020).

As these cases make clear, passive surveillance bots pose a substantial threat to individual privacy and human rights. An actor doesn't need access to classified information or private data to learn invasively intimate details about an individual; the amount of legally and publicly available data on any given individual on the web is substantial and growing by the day, and it's extremely easy for bots to collate and triangulate that data to create very detailed and scarily accurate profiles. The process of culling information from publicly available sources and analyzing and collating it is known as *open-source intelligence* (OSINT). The time and skill required to produce good OSINT analysis is substantial, but the private companies and governments that have the resources to do it are willing to make the investment; the former deputy director of the CIA has called for the creation of a US intelligence agency devoted exclusively to OSINT collection and analysis (Zegart & Morell, 2019).

The collective amount of data that humanity has produced – the *digital universe* – is, like the physical universe, ever-expanding – growing at an exponential rate. In a future world where the amount of publicly available data exceeds hundreds of zettabytes, bots will be a key tool for automating OSINT data collection and analysis. Zhenhua and Clearview AI poignantly illustrate that bots will play a key role in this world, and that their threat to individual privacy is substantial. How can we responsibly use bots for necessary data collection in the future while not violating civil and digital liberties? This will be a difficult question for companies, governments, and citizens in the future.

Active surveillance – transparency

Of course, not all surveillance is quiet. Some bots designed to surveil other users or websites actively push the information they find into the public domain. Transparency bots, or "automated agents that use social media to draw attention to the behavior of particular [political] actors," fall into this category (McKelvey & Dubois, 2017). At times, transparency can be a decidedly unsexy and monotonous affair. It's often a form of activism dedicated to meticulously recording mundane events and raw data: documenting who met with whom, who went where, who said what, who edited or censored whom, etc. As we've seen already, bots excel at this kind of work. Unlike humans, their attention is truly unwavering. Bots record and oversee what happens on computers and servers all around the world every day. Wikipedia bots, for example, keep track of what edits have taken place, as well as the details of the edits (who made them, at what time, and from what IP address). Logging these changes is one of their main functions (Gorwa, 2017b).

The information logged by Wikipedia bots is publicly available and can be used for other purposes. A particularly creative and transparency-oriented use for this public data is the "WikiEdits bots," a series of Twitter bots that kept track of Wikipedia edits from official governmental IP addresses around the world, trying to catch government offices engaging in subtle PR or propaganda (Ford, Dubois, et al., 2016). These bots appeared in countries around the world, including @Parliamentedits (UK), @AussieParlEdits (Australia), @CongressEdits (USA), @GCCAedits (Canada), @RiksdagWikiEdit (Sweden). These bots send public tweets whenever edits are made to Wikipedia pages from governmental IP addresses, alerting the public whenever governments may be altering Wikipedia pages for their own benefit (Butler, 2019; Cox, 2014). These bots therefore serve as a deterrent for underhanded governmental officials who may want to strategically bend the truth – the US-based @CongressEdits bot helped uncover a congressional staffer's attempts to sanitize the Wikipedia page on the "Torture Report," a document that revealed details of CIA human rights abuses in the War on Terror to the American public for the first time (Ries, 2014).

A similar project is the "Dictator Alert" Twitter bots, which track the flights of autocrats in and out of airports around the world (Toor, 2016), creating a "paper trail" from which information about clandestine meetings with other leaders can be derived. Bots like these enhance the public's ability to shine a spotlight on events that may otherwise remain out of sight.

Social activism – The dawn of the bots populi

As transparency bots show, automation can be used to serve the people. Bots are an important tool for grassroots activists, who use them to hypercharge activism and political engagement. Almost without exception, individuals and organizations engaged in social and political activism lack the resources and manpower necessary to bring about the change they envision, and activism requires resources: to work, activism must engage the broader public and spread the message. Being short on manpower, time, or money, many civil society activists have turned to bots to amplify their message cheaply and quickly.

"Botivist," a short-lived academic experiment, showed how bots can usefully support activism. This Spanish-language botnet, run by a group of scholars, was used to post anti-corruption messages, introduce activists to each other, and test communication strategies among activists – activities aimed at increasing anti-corruption activism in Latin America. In its eleven-day lifespan, Botivist generated 1,236 interactions among activists on Twitter (Savage et al., 2015).

Other social activism bots have been created by programmers working completely on their own. Nigel Leck, an Australian programmer and climate activist, built @AI_AGW (*"Artificial Intelligence: Anthropogenic Climate Change"*). The bot, which debuted in 2008, was one of the first activist bots on the Twitter platform, and its aim was "hunting down false claims made by climate change deniers, calling them out, and correcting them with information linked from peer-reviewed essays in scientific research journals" (Swanstrom, 2019). The bot used keyword detection and pattern matching (similar to ELIZA) to detect tweets that denied climate change, then responded with relevant scientific literature. Part of Leck's motivation in creating the bot was pure fatigue – he was tired of having the same arguments with climate change skeptics over and over, and so (in typical engineer fashion) he automated the job. The bot ground away in the trenches of climate change arguments for four years, but was banned by Twitter in 2012 (Mims, 2010; Swanstrom, 2019).

Although enormous numbers of bots are being used to spread disinformation, civil society has also created bots to fight disinformation. Cofacts, a civic tech project that grew out of the hacktivist collective gOv.tw ("gov zero") in Taiwan, is one of the most innovative uses of bots to emerge in the past decade. After a wave of false news stories inundated Taiwan in 2018, activists Johnson Liang and Billion Lee built a bot that collected user-reported suspicious stories, sent the stories to human volunteers to fact-check them, then sent the findings back to the reporting user. The bot runs on the encrypted chat app LINE, a popular messaging app in Taiwan similar to WhatsApp. To report stories, users simply add the bot and send it links to suspicious news stories (Monaco, 2017).

Pro-democracy activists have also used bots in the wild to promote causes and politicians. Opposition activists in Russia, Ukraine, and Venezuela have deployed bots as a democratic organization tool (Forelle et al., 2015; Stukal et al., 2019).[2] Cases like these illustrate bots' dual nature: bots can be used for good or ill, depending on who is using them – governments, corporations, or grassroots actors – and for what purposes. Ultimately, bots reflect the intentions of their builders and users.

The Bot Arms Race

In the past decade, we have become all too aware of the ubiquity and effectiveness of political bots. As we've seen, they have been used to lend an illusion of support to politicians and political campaigns; to attempt to influence voter behavior; to harass dissidents and censor independent media outlets; and to megaphone both grassroots and astroturfed political speech. Many of these bots are very simple, programmed by amateurs using code available online. Some, however, are growing more sophisticated. To have a chance of doing the work they are designed to do, bots have been forced to evolve far beyond the Usenet and IRC bots of the early 1990s. As platforms beef up their security and their bot detection systems, bot builders must continue to step up their game to evade these new measures – a kind of bot "arms race" between bot builders and bot detectors. Interestingly, the same actor may wear both hats at different times. Many private companies work to prevent scraping on their sites while deploying bots to scrape data on competitors' platforms (Foote, 2018). To some extent, this is part of a long tradition in the hacking and cybersecurity world. Illicit hackers (people who hack for their own gain, known as "black hats") often change teams, becoming "white hats," who use their previous hacking experience to test for (and patch) the same kinds of vulnerabilities that they had previously exploited.

There is a highly successful new weapon in this bot arms race: the cyborg, which moves away from the completely automated bot (easily detected) to the partially automated bot/human hybrid profile (much more difficult to identify). Cyborgs' hybrid nature allows them to evade current bot detection systems.

One successful cyborg account was @McYangin, a Twitter account devoted to promoting presidential hopeful Andrew Yang in the Democratic primary. @McYangin combined manual and automated activity to boost Yang-related hashtags. The Digital Intelligence Lab at Institute for the Future found that the account retweeted #YangGang and similar hashtags over 2,600 times in September 2019 (the month of the democratic presidential primary debate). The same month, a different cyborg account retweeted anti-vax disinformation, hoping users would buy antivax merchandise from the account's operator (Monaco, 2019b).

Cyborgs are also difficult to recognize when they are part of what is known as a *volunteer botnet*. These cyborg networks are made up of real human user accounts, recruited (knowingly or unknowingly) into a political botnet. These botnets turn real human accounts into cyborgs by automating some of their posting activity. In volunteer botnets, campaigns recruit users to volunteer to allow their accounts to send some automated tweets promoting a candidate. (In a more sinister version of this, user accounts can be temporarily hijacked to post campaign tweets – some apps ask users to approve app permissions that are overly broad, and users can accidentally give permission for bots to post tweets on their behalf.) The volunteer botnet is an extremely powerful tool for campaigns, particularly if it is used sparingly. Thousands of accounts whose activity is normally extremely diverse can be activated to send the same tweet at a given time, creating an illusion of extremely strong support from a large swath of diverse human users. Volunteer botnets have been used by the Russian government and by political campaigns in Italy and Mexico (Woolley & Monaco, 2020). With these volunteer botnets, political campaigns can exploit the ability of cyborgs to fly under platforms' bot detection radar, spreading their message and manufacturing consensus in a way that seems organic rather than manipulated.

Cyborgs and volunteer botnets need not be nefarious; grassroots activists have used them to boost voter turnout. In the United Kingdom's 2017 snap elections, Tinder cyborgs were used to increase turnout for the Labour party. In this volunteer botnet, willing volunteers "donated" their profiles to be controlled by bots on the popular dating app Tinder for two hours at a time. The bot would use a set of pre-defined criteria to attempt to persuade voters between 18 and 25 years of age to vote for the Labour party in the upcoming election. The team behind the bot estimated it sent between 30,000 and 40,000 messages to 18–25-year-olds in marginal constituencies, with the explicit goal of *"oust[ing] the conservative government."* The tactic gained positive coverage in the press and seemed to work; the age group targeted by the Tinder bot displayed its highest election turnout since 1992 (Fowler & Goodman, 2017; Rasmussen, 2017).

The bot arms race – platforms' attempts to curb bot activity and the corresponding evolutions in political bot technology – are here to stay and will likely intensify. By the end of the 2010s, researchers working in the disinformation space had largely convinced the public and social media platforms that bots and disinformation campaigns had the potential to do great harm to political participation, discourse, and organizing. In industry, government, and academia alike, disinformation experts were looking for solutions to the bot- and cyborg-driven computational propaganda problem. Great progress has been made since 2016, but solutions to the problem are still experimental, and bot designers continue to match each change with another technological leap to evade new strictures.

And, unlike many political bot designers (whose only concern is whether they are making money and/or gaining power), the counter-propagandists and "white-hat" bot designers looking for solutions to the bot problem must grapple with the ethics of their counter-disinformation campaigns. Tradeoffs are inescapable. Collecting large amounts of data can shed light on the tradecraft and techniques behind disinformation campaigns, but data collection at this scale presents problems of violating user privacy. Similarly, when social media platforms increase their transparency by revealing information about their proactive detection and deplatforming techniques, it increases user trust, but this also lets bad actors see behind the curtain, giving them information that could help them evade these countermeasures. Even some uses of bots that seem at first glance to be positive, such as identifying and limiting hate speech on social platforms, involve tradeoffs. These propositions are much easier in theory than in practice: algorithmic detection of hate speech is a difficult computational problem that varies by language, culture, and region; on top of that, the limitation of speech online raises complex ethical, legal, and social issues.

There are inherent tradeoffs in any solution to the problem of political bots and disinformation, and we think that it is a mistake to go too far in either direction. To address the problem of political bots, we recommend relatively moderate measures: increasing data sharing among social media companies and trusted expert partners; passing specific regulations against particular uses of bots (such as for political campaigning), but not against bots themselves; and requiring more transparency in political funding, including political advertising online (Monaco & Woolley, 2017).

Conclusion

Perhaps it was impossible for us to have foreseen the impact that bots would have on cultural, social, and political life. It was not until very recently that social media companies realized (or admitted) the damage that political bots and astroturfing were doing on their platforms. In 2016, a spokesperson for Twitter bluntly said: "Anyone claiming that spam accounts on Twitter are distorting the national political conversation is misinformed" (Schreckinger, 2016). The same year, Facebook founder and CEO Mark Zuckerberg dismissed the idea that disinformation could have an influence on elections as "pretty crazy" – a stance he admitted to regretting a mere ten months later (Solon, 2016; Zuckerberg, 2017).

But we must remember that the bots are not the problem. The problem is the people behind the bots. In the end, political disinformation is always spread by humans, who design, orchestrate, and organize these campaigns. Bots simply carry them out. As we've seen, bots can amplify speech, game algorithms, censor political positions through dampening and DDoS attacks, collect data online, surveil targets, and influence voter behavior. But they can also increase transparency, streamline the fact-checking process, and increase democratic participation and engagement.

Bots have been around since the early days of the internet, and they're here to stay. No matter how much companies, legislators, and activists fight to counteract their nefarious uses, they will continue to exist on social media in the future. They will also continue to evolve, in both miraculous-seeming and deeply concerning ways. One of the extremely worrisome developments in the realm of automated disinformation is the "deepfake" technologies – synthetic media that allow bots and computer programs to create incredibly realistic-seeming videos, audio, and images out of thin air. One of the most exciting developments is the rapid advancements in natural language processing and the simulation of human conversation, which have led to new, more advanced chatbots like GPT-3. Without proper platform design, regulation, and planning, these tools – and the newer, more powerful ones that will inevitably succeed them – could hypercharge the harms that bots run by bad actors can wreak on democracy (Watts & Hwang, 2020). How harmful bots will be in the future, and how resilient we are to malicious abuse of these technologies, depends in large part upon what we do now. To properly respond to the threat posed by political bots, we need to work out how to craft sensible policies and regulations.

4
Bots and Commerce

In early spring of 2016, Microsoft released a Twitter bot they named Tay, an AI chatbot built to emulate a nineteen-year-old American girl. Microsoft's Twitter description of Tay called her an "AI with zero chill." According to the @TayandYou description, "the more you talk the smarter Tay gets"[1] (Microsoft, 2016a). It was Tay's capacity to learn from those she talked to that was her undoing. In designing Tay, Microsoft failed to consider the irreverence of certain corners of the internet, which are full of people who'll do anything for the lulz. They also failed to consider the darker urges roiling in other corners of the internet, which are full of people dying for an opportunity to spread racism, sexism, and intolerance.

These groups converged on Tay. Almost as soon as she was released, Tay learned from the tweets she was reading and began tweeting hate-laden messages. This quickly snowballed. As other Twitter users realized that the bot wasn't pre-programmed to avoid such content, they began sending it more and more offensive and bigoted messages. Again, she learned from these messages and emulated them, intensifying her racist and sexually charged rhetoric. Zero chill indeed.

Tay tweeted nearly 100,000 times in her first (and only) day of existence; Microsoft suspended her account after only sixteen hours to make adjustments. They wrote that they "had prepared for many types of abuses of the system," but it seems quite plain that they hadn't prepared for Twitter; they blamed Tay's rapid decompensation on "a coordinated attack by a subset of people [who] exploited a vulnerability" in the bot

(P. Lee, 2016). When Microsoft accidentally re-released Tay on Twitter a few days later (Graham, 2016), she was quickly sending out drug-related tweets and spamming hundreds of thousands of followers with repetitive messages. They quickly yanked her account again, this time for good.

What did Tay's builders learn from this gargantuan blunder? According to Microsoft CEO Sadya Nadella, Tay changed the way they designed going forward: "one of the things that has really influenced our design principles is that episode, we have to take accountability." According to her, the "first and foremost" lesson they learned was that "we need to be able to in fact foresee these attacks" (Shepard, 2017). Microsoft's release of Tay without considering how the account could be gamed by malicious users speaks to a systemic problem with technology companies: they innovate first and ask questions about social impact later – as Mark Zuckerberg infamously put it, they "move fast and break things." Despite the Tay debacle, said Nadella, AI – and particularly conversational AI – remained one of the "three pillars" of Microsoft's future strategy, along with quantum computing and mixed reality (Shepard); by the time Tay was released, the company had already invested massive amounts of resources into the type of conversational AI that Tay represented. (Cortana, a digital personal assistant programmed into many Microsoft devices and programs, is another example of Microsoft's conversational AI at work.) What did they really learn? And what can we learn about how business – the profit motive – drives bot development, and how little it cares about social consequences?

For many tech companies, 2016 was the year of the bot (Bruner, 2016). Bots – and particularly conversational AI bots – were seen as the future of user interface; soon after (and despite) the failure of Tay, Nadella boldly told attendees at that year's Microsoft Build Conference that "bots are the new apps" (Reynolds, 2016). O'Reilly media explained that, "consumers are comfortable with conversational interfaces, and AI has finally progressed to the point where it can offer useful responses to practical queries." Their paean to bots shows business's real interest in them: profit. According to O'Reilly,

> Bots promise to inject information, intelligence, and online services into just about any scenario [...] Bots will give workers superpowers, make networks more accessible, reorder user experiences, and build new ecosystems. And they promise developers a faster way into users' pockets as the app economy matures. (Bruner)

As Microsoft worked to make its bot dreams – led by Cortana and XiaoIce[2] – come to life, its competitors were doing the same. Around that time, Facebook talked about shifting management of user experience on its Messenger platform to an all-inclusive AI assistant named "M" (Olanaff & Constine, 2015). Amazon's Alexa, Apple's Siri, and Google Assistant were thriving. The messenger app Kik went all in on bot-driven advertising (Mims, 2014). But, just two years later, in early January 2018, *Wired* magazine ran the headline "Facebook's Virtual Assistant M Is Dead. So Are Chatbots" (Griffith & Simonite, 2018). The public's attitude toward bots had flipped in the aftermath of the political bot-laden debacle of the 2016 US election and UK Brexit referendum, and between this and the fallout from Tay, many companies began to feel the term "bot" was poisoned. They began rebranding the concept, shifting away from the term "bot" and toward the broader idea of "AI."

But as we know at this point in the book, at their core, conversational AIs are still chatbots. Even dressed up with new names – "AI" or "virtual" assistants or some other Silicon Valley buzz-phrase du jour – bots of all types are so central to the way we interact with the digital world that they are not going anywhere. And as the digital world grows ever more central to every aspect of daily life, especially to business and finance, bots will continue to grow more and more commercially valuable.

In this chapter, we discuss what we will broadly call "business bots," or commercial bots: bots that support the daily work and long-term economic goals of companies. These types of bots include high-frequency trading bots in finance, customer service bots, digital personal assistants that make technology more and more necessary to potential customers, spambots, messaging app bots aimed at innovatively selling products, scraper bots that gather data to help inform marketing and product development, social bots (like Tay) designed to market a business and its products, and helper bots that improve users' interactions with red tape and bureaucracy – or, in truth, improve the outcomes of those interactions for the businesses that use them. As with other bots, they are crucial to the functioning of the hyperconnected modern business world. They might operate in the background, aiding in automated trading processes or bank transactions, but our current global financial system would have a hard time operating in their absence.

Some of these commerce or business bots, such as XiaoIce, Tay, and many others, operate through social media platforms' application programming interfaces (APIs). We discuss how these APIs allow commercial bots to gather data on consumers (just as political bot makers gathered information on voters) and interact directly with consumers online. We end this chapter with a discussion of Tim Berners-Lee's utopian conception of the "Semantic Web," a system of networked devices, grounded on bots and APIs, that carry out the mundane and formulaic tasks of daily life in order to free up humans' time, allowing them the freedom to do tasks that they find meaningful (Berners-Lee et al., 2001; Alpaydin, 2016).

What Is a Business Bot?

At bottom, most commercial bots are designed to allow businesses to automate transactions with consumers, clients, partners, and other entities. For instance, rather than relying on a human representative, a company can invest in an automated agent geared toward providing support or services to a potential customer. Even Tay, who was not directly tied to any point-of-sale or direct marketing function, was conceived as a sort of marketing exhibit for Microsoft's AI work. Some business bots are user-facing bots, similar to those we have discussed in the chapters on social and political bots. These bots are connected to the internet, and they can communicate with users: in text, via a chatroom-style interface, by speaking aloud to users, like Cortana or Siri; or even by using cursors and other mechanisms to show users where to access resources or how to do certain things on a given website or platform.

But not all business bots have a forward-facing, interactive, customer-service function. In fact, it's safe to say that the majority of business bots never directly interact with consumers. Most are built to do behind-the-scenes work, such as searching for and parsing useful financial data and conducting automatic stock trades based on that information. The website "Botnerds," a useful repository of all things bot, outlines a number of different ways that businesses and other groups can use automated online software (botnerds, 2020). They provide detailed information on the two main types of business bots: business to consumer (B2C) bots and business to business (B2B) bots. They also categorize business bots into "good bots" and "bad bots." On the "good" side there are the business versions of some familiar bots: the crawler bots that we discussed in Chapter 1 and business-focused versions of chatbots, introduced in Chapter 2 and discussed as social bots in Chapter 3. Other "good" business bots are transactional bots, informational bots, and entertainment bots. On the "bad" side there are hackers, spammers, scrapers, and impersonators.

Crawlers or **spiders**, which we discussed in Chapter 1, are bots built to run automatically behind the scenes, seeking out and cataloguing information from websites and APIs. They have myriad uses in business. Google, for instance – one of the most valuable businesses in the world – is built around its marquee product, a search engine based on a web crawler, the Google bot. The Google bot is "designed to be run simultaneously by thousands of machines to improve performance and scale as the web grows" (Google, 2020a) to seek out new webpages online. From there, the bot "visits, or crawls, the page to find out what's on it. Google renders the page and analyzes both the text and non-text content and overall visual layout to decide where it should appear in Search results" (Google, 2020b). As you might imagine, people long to know how to attract the Google Bot's attention and to game the search results algorithm that ranks each site. Tips and tricks for "SEO" (search engine optimization) abound online, and some consulting firms charge top dollar for advice on how to design websites to get them near the top of Google searches. The same is true for Microsoft's search engine Bing, which uses its – you guessed it – Bing Bot in a similar capacity. Crawlers are also used by businesses for many other purposes: keeping tabs on the price of goods across various sites, for example, or checking for software updates or bug reports for critical digital infrastructure.

Transactional bots can be used on business websites on both the front-end (the customer-facing side of the site) or the back-end (the behind-the-scenes side that carries out company business, such as tracking stock, running credit card charges, sending vendor updates, etc.). Front-end bots are usually built to support data exchanges directly with consumers: a bank might use a transactional bot rather than a human customer service agent to confirm a wire transfer or verify a customer's identity, or a local gas company might use a bot to provide a quote for service based upon certain inputs, such as address and type of service requested. While these bots are similar in some ways to customer service chatbots, these bots are programmed to carry out discrete, specific tasks. Back-end bots support similar data exchanges, sending and retrieving data for various parties; the back-end bots may make these exchanges with other websites, businesses, or business bots. For example, a bank bot might communicate with another bank's bot to actually carry out a funds transfer, or a gas company bot might receive automatic updates from their suppliers about changes in gas prices or transport delays. (We discuss one specific type of transactional bot, the finance bot, in more depth below.)

Informational (info) bots are designed to give connected users information, tips, and helpful suggestions. These bits of content might be delivered directly to your cell phone or tablet through a push notification, or they might be delivered inside a messaging service like Slack or WhatsApp. Sometimes you might query a given info bot by writing a specific command into the chat line. On Discord, for instance, users can query weather bot about the seven-day forecast in a given region by typing the command: !weather week [zipcode]. There are many types of info bots, built to operate across a wide range of communication platforms. Social media and chat applications' informational bots may be made in-house by their own companies, or they may integrate bots by third-party businesses. Informational bots range from those built to curate news for users (Breaking News Bot shares emerging media stories on Slack, GamerBot shares gaming news on Messenger, CNN bot shares CNN news stories on Kik) to those aimed at helping you decide what's for dinner (give the Messenger bot Dinner Ideas a list of what's in your fridge and pantry and it will tell you what to cook).

Entertainment bots are everywhere online, and they are big business. From comedy bots that automatically share jokes to art bots that use various data to produce digital images and video game bots that farm in-game resources, entertainment bots can generate income for their builders. For example, a video game bot to automate resource farming in Minecraft might be sold by the designer, either for a direct one-time cost or a subscription fee. A builder of an art bot or comedy bot might use it as an automated influencer, generating money via views, likes, or clicks and clever use of advertisements or by marketing particular products, just like human influencers on Instagram. Recently, automated avatars – animated versions of artists, actors, or musicians run by automated bots – have become popular with celebrities. An automated avatar from a company like Genies can allow Justin Bieber or Cardi B to "appear" on a digital platform without actually having to be there in person (Phan, 2021).

In addition to this list of what botnerds call "good" business bots, there are also many "bad" business bots – if they are profitable, some businesses will use them. Many businesses sell or use bots to illicitly scrape information or hack competitors. The infamous digital political firm Cambridge Analytica allegedly used scrapers – a violation of Facebook's terms of service – to gather information on US users before the 2016 US presidential election (Wong, 2019). Many businesses use hacker bots to spread malware, malicious software that is designed to damage the digital assets of those who fall prey to it. Some companies use bots in DDoS attacks to take down their competition's websites. Many companies still use spam bots (which most of us are all too familiar with!) to send out automated marketing garbage, trying to sell you pharmaceuticals via email or to peddle knock-off fashions on Twitter. And finally, some companies deploy what are known as impersonator bots, which mimic real people, in order to manipulate a given target. Impersonator bots are also used for political purposes, as when real people's identities are used to send automated messages in order to sway public opinion on behalf of a government, military, or corporate client. But, on the purely commercial side, impersonator bots are used to carry out frauds, stealing a person's identity on a social media platform and then using that fake profile to shake down friends and family members or make fraudulent purchases.

Business Chatbots and Customer Service

Chatbots were described in their social role in Chapter 2, which explores the social use of bots. However, not all chatbots are social bots; there are also business-owned and -operated chatbots like XiaoIce and Tay. As you've undoubtedly noticed in your own daily life, many businesses are beginning to replace human customer service agents with chatbots, both in text-based support and phone support. Most of us have interacted with commercial bots, because most any contact with a big business, like your bank or insurance company, first happens through a bot. Lose your debit card or want to check on your deductible? Maybe you're waiting on a shipment from FedEx or a delivery from an online florist? You call the business or log onto their website and click on the online "help desk" and – hey presto! – you're talking to a bot. These experiences don't always go well. Audio-enabled bots regularly mishear you or pick up background noise: you say "Give me customer service" and they respond, "Did you ask, how do I work this?" There are problems with text-based bots, too: they have very limited capabilities, and if your issue is remotely complex, you're likely in for a long wait to talk to a human being who can actually help.

Some of these bots work beautifully, but others – well, not so much. Innovations in AI and machine learning have allowed for more sophisticated commercial chatbot interfaces, but debacles like the Tay fiasco still happen, and there are certainly countless badly programmed interfaces. Although many customer service bots are undeniably annoying, they are getting better. Companies are putting serious money into automated transactional bots and digital personal assistants, and at financial institutions, retail outlets, medical organizations, and other types of companies, customer service bots are now the first point of contact for most customers. On the businesses' side, the appeal of bots is clear: bots are cheaper to employ than human service agents, they are always on call, and they can be programmed to do all kinds of things, sometimes even better than humans could. According to *Business Insider*, chatbots are now "vital" to companies' customer service channels (Nguyen, 2020) because of their "efficiency" and 24/7 convenience. They say that bots are "revolutionizing the way companies stay with customers by giving customers the ability to contact the company through messaging apps, email, or text to help foster brand loyalty." The idea, they suggest, is that good-quality customer service bots can keep a potential customer engaged and on the hook, while bad customer service, from humans or from bots, can easily drive them off: just "a single negative customer service experience can deter potential customers from a company," and 60 percent of consumers in the US have decided not to buy something they intended to because of experiencing bad customer service.[3]

Transactional Bots and Finance

Bots are deeply and intimately related not only to commerce itself – its infrastructure, and increasingly, its workforce – but are inextricably wound up with finance and the way that money circulates within finance markets, and thus within the global economy. Financial (or "trading") bots structure the socio-technical intricacies of finance and trading. As Mackenzie (2008) points out, financial markets are supported and altered by both the structures and theories that surround them; derivatives futures trading wouldn't have skyrocketed in the late 1990s and early 2000s without legitimization from particular economic theorization, and markets wouldn't function as they do without the code – and bots – that underlie them. As Geiger (Geiger, 2014) has said of Wikipedia, a "'minimally regulated' [...] environment rests on top of a wide variety of bespoke code that has been specifically developed and deployed to produce, sustain, and enforce particular understandings of what 'the wiki way' [or we might also say 'the market'] is and ought to be" (p. 353).

But what do bots *do* in the financial markets? As with other bots we have seen, they generally either automate repetitive tasks or deal with volumes of data that humans could not manage, collecting and analyzing huge amounts of information very rapidly. As with other commercial bots, financial bots automate a good deal of boring maintenance work, recording trades, sending automatic financial reports to the SEC, etc. But their real value to the financial markets lies in the second set of tasks: collecting, analyzing, and acting at speed on massive volumes of information – the bread and butter of the financial markets.

There are three types of bots doing this latter type of work. The first type of bots, simulation trading bots, run trading scenarios against actual historical price data, testing the success of various potential investing strategies. The second type of bots, execution-oriented trade bots, automatically carry out particular types of trades whenever certain pre-programmed trigger conditions are met – when particular stocks reach a certain price, or undergo a certain number of trades in a set period of time. The third type of bots are "arbitrage bots," which monitor and compare the price of currencies across various exchanges and make trades based upon favorable rates.[4]

These trading bots are controversial, and many economists argue that their use has changed the way markets work in a fundamental way – some think for the better, some think for the worse. According to Park and Wang (2020), because trading bots "monitor prices in major securities closely and continuously, increase their quoting activities significantly and cause individual stocks' returns to align more closely with the market," their use helped to resurrect the capital asset pricing model, which is used by financial planners and others to determine acceptable return rates on assets. In other words, these bots are able to keep track of the stock market in such a way that they can more accurately help people determine how much money they will make or lose – and whether the risks they are taking are more or less reasonable. Park and Wang's analysis of the S&P 500 index shows that when "electronic, automated trading" debuted ten years ago in US markets, it fundamentally altered the market – and not just in the US – by causing massive changes to trading speed and, therefore, people's ability to parse particular aspects of the market such as return rates on specific stocks.

Others (Borch, 2016) have pointed out the downsides of trading bots. Algorithm-driven bots can engage in high-frequency trading (HFT) – "fully automated, superfast computerized trading" (p. 350). According to Borch, this high-frequency trading is "prone to run amok in unanticipated frenzy," because it moves too fast for normal humans to notice and intervene when things go wrong, and errors compound at lightning speed. This contributed to the 2010 "Flash Crash," when broad-scale HFT by brokers taking advantage of loopholes in new US financial regulations led to a trillion-dollar stock market crash in around thirty minutes.

Despite this, automated trading appears to be here to stay. According to risk management expert Aaron Brown (2020), former managing director and head of financial market research at AQR Capital Management, "HFT will be as important a force in the 2020s as it was in the previous decades." HFT is no longer the Wild West of finance markets, and regulations now govern its use, making it more difficult for investors to engage in imprudent, risky behavior via HFT. Almost certainly, then, the bots that facilitate HFT are also here to stay. As AI progresses, these bots could be programmed to be much smarter when it comes to measuring such risks. But finance bots, like all other bots, have *people* behind them – and the flaws in those people (or the flaws in their bot-building methods or their economic theories or even their ethical compass) could produce serious problems for the commercial sector.

Conclusion

As Tim Berners-Lee predicted, the internet has become integral to our daily lives, helping ease the burden of mundane, repetitive tasks in many ways. The system of networked devices that he calls the Semantic Web can reduce the burdens of bureaucracy and allow us more time to do things we love. Remember the DoNotPay bot from Chapter 1? Originally designed to simplify the process of contesting a parking ticket, DoNotPay developed into an automated service that helped users easily navigate a wide array of legal and bureaucratic processes, including automatically canceling free trials or subscriptions, fighting email spam, and processing refunds (Mannes, 2019). Billed as "the world's first robot lawyer," DoNotPay claims to allow people to "fight corporations, beat bureaucracy, and sue anyone at the press of a button" (DoNotPay, 2021). The DoNotPay bot (which is, in fact, a commercial bot) seems to encapsulate Berners-Lee's dream – to realize the best version of the internet, helping humans to live more meaningful lives.

But the worst version of the internet is equally realized; remember that trolls taught Tay racism, misogyny, and hatred in only sixteen hours, all for the lulz. Clearly, we've got work to do. Perhaps the time is right; in the aftermath of the 2016 political bot reckoning, these companies – not just social media, but all kinds of internet platforms – are increasingly under fire for their focus on profit above people. Politicians and the public are fired up about the antisocial effects the internet is having on all aspects of our lives. Perhaps now is the time to demand change. We can design our platforms with happiness and contentedness in mind, and with democracy and human rights coded into their processes (Woolley, 2020b).

To move toward this vision of the Semantic Web, however, the constituent parts of the internet – social media, journalism and politics, commerce – should be constructed to benefit society and people rather than line their founders' and shareholders' pockets. Currently, most social media sites are optimized to keep us on their platform rather than encourage us to go outside or spend quality time offline with a friend. These platforms want us to see adverts and buy stuff and, as long as we keep doing that, they don't care if we are happy. Finance and trading bots are currently underregulated and may continue to cause market strife, which most strongly affects the poorest among us, not those who could afford to invest in stock. The corporate sector must consider the human cost of rushing into automating customer service. Yes, customer service chatbots and virtual personal assistants are convenient for people who need help at odd hours of the night. But these bots are most often used because they benefit the company, not the customer. Bots replace human workers because they are cheaper – they don't need health insurance, or paid time off, or parental leave. Perhaps companies rushing to invest in automation should remember Business Insider's (2020) claim that poor customer service drives people away; most people would agree that humans do customer service jobs more effectively than any automated machine ever could, for humans (unlike bots) can understand emotions like frustration, sadness, and anger.

5
Bots and Artificial Intelligence

"How are you adjusting to all your new-found fame?" the interviewer asked.

Eugene Goostman's response was a little cagey: "I would rather not talk about it if you don't mind. By the way, what's your occupation? I mean – could you tell me about your work?" (Aamoth, 2014).

Eugene was having a hard time getting used to the limelight. Or maybe he wasn't. Becoming famous overnight would pose its challenges for any thirteen-year-old boy, but Eugene's attempt to dodge the question was not informed by a sense of teenage social angst: it's not that Eugene was having trouble understanding or talking about his feelings, it was simply that he didn't have any. But to expose this fact would have run counter to the entire goal of the Eugene Goostman program: convince anyone who talks to you that you are a human, not a bot mimicking a human.

Eugene wasn't perfect, but it seemed that he was perfect enough. In June 2014, according to some press releases, he became the "first" bot to allegedly pass the Turing test. The test is named after one of the founding fathers of AI, Alan Turing, who came up with it in 1950 to make obsolete the question "can machines think?" According to Turing, if a machine is able to carry out a task with results indistinguishable from those achieved by a human, it doesn't matter whether the machine is thinking (Wooldridge, 2020, p. 236). For example, if a machine were skilled enough to convince a conversational partner that it was human, that means that the machine's conversational results are functionally the same as those of a human, regardless of whether the machine is actually "thinking" (Sharkey, 2012; Turing, 1950). This is exactly what Eugene Goostman was able to do in the *Turing Test 2014* competition held at the Royal Society in London. In typed conversation through a computer terminal, Eugene successfully fooled 33 percent of judges into believing it was human (BBC News, 2014).

How did he do it? For one thing, his mimicry of human conversation was successful within constraints on expectations, produced by a biographical sleight of hand: Eugene said that he was a thirteen-year-old Ukrainian boy. Many of Eugene's Turing test conversational partners missed telltale bot errors because they ascribed them to his speaking English as a second language, or to the fact that short attention spans and non-sequiturs aren't exactly rare among teenage boys.

The event's organizers at the University of Reading hailed Eugene's accomplishments as "historic" and "a milestone in artificial intelligence" (University of Reading, 2014), and many participants felt the same. But not everyone was on board. The event organizers said that Eugene had passed the Turing test chatting freely, with no pre-defined topics, but others said that "Eugene Goostman proves the power of fakery; it's a tour de force of clever engineering, but a long way from genuine intelligence," (Marcus, 2014). Other experts in the field have rightly pointed out that early bots like PARRY, which operated in a similarly constrained conversational environment, passed the Turing test as far back as 1972 (Jurafsky & Martin, 2020). PARRY was a basic chatbot that imitated paranoid schizophrenics, and psychologists were unable to distinguish transcripts of interviews with PARRY from transcripts of interviews with real human patients who actually suffered from the disease (Colby et al., 1972) – in part because (like teenage boys) paranoid schizophrenics often jump topics or deliver non-sequiturs.

According to Hugh Loebner, an American inventor and AI enthusiast, the particular instance of the Turing test passed by Eugene was not valid because the conversations only lasted five minutes; he argued that judges could not make an informed conclusion about their conversational partners in that time (Bosker, 2014). Loebner himself was a long-time organizer of an annual Turing Test competition known as *The Loebner Prize*, in which judges conversed for 25 minutes with their partners at the terminal. In previous years, Eugene hadn't succeeded in Loebner's competition. But even Loebner's competition is not universally seen as valid among AI experts. According to Marvin Minsky, one of the pioneering founders of AI, Loebner's competition was "obnoxious and stupid" and "a meaningless publicity stunt" (Sundman, 2003; Wooldridge, 2020, p. 27). Still other experts dismiss Eugene's win because they find the Turing Test itself an outdated and arbitrary hurdle. As one journalist put it: "passing the Turing Test is less about building machines intelligent enough to convince humans they're real and more about building programs that can anticipate certain questions from humans in order to pre-form and return semi-intelligible answers" (Aamoth, 2014).

The Eugene Goostman saga embodies many of the themes that run through the history of AI. Since AI emerged as a concept, press about AI progress has often been sensational and misleading; experts have often disagreed about what constitutes "intelligence" and how we can get there; and it has always been easier to build task-specific programs that succeed in tightly circumscribed contexts than to design general-purpose machines that can adapt and perform well in many situations.

In this chapter, we'll explore these and other themes as we dig into the history of AI, particularly in relation to bots. AI is a broad field with a rich history that draws on philosophy, linguistics, sociology, and computer science, recently broadening to include statistics and probability and even neuroscience. It covers everything from computer vision to robotic vacuums. Though the subject is a fascinating one in its own right, we'll zoom in on events and developments – particularly those in the AI subfield of machine learning – that have been most relevant to bot evolution and bots' recent turn to using AI. We'll explore how bots use AI to converse with humans and even detect other bots, and briefly survey future developments in AI that could drive the next bot revolution.

These developments will show both how much bots have advanced with recent AI developments, but also how few of them truly make use of AI techniques – even when newspapers or companies claim that they do. All the same, AI techniques have enhanced human–bot communication and have driven evolution in political, social, and commerce bot technologies in recent years. To boot, AI techniques enhance bots' understanding of the real world, such as the actual meanings of words in a sentence, and hold great promise to enhance both bot-to-bot and bot-to-human communication.

What Is AI?

Just like bots, AI is difficult to define. AI is often a moving target, not a matter of uniform consensus among AI developers. Technology historian Paul Ceruzzi offers a useful basic definition: "the classic definition [of AI] is that of a computer that performs actions that, if done by a human being, would be considered intelligent." But however useful, Ceruzzi himself notes this is not a stable classifier, for "In practice, as computers become more powerful, actions such as playing a good game of chess are no longer considered AI, although they once were considered at the forefront of AI research" (Ceruzzi, 2012, p. 169).

The slipperiness of the definition is also partly due to hype (or sometimes even outright deceit) from disingenuous developers. Some of what is touted as AI is simply smoke and mirrors. Historically, the first "AI," the late nineteenth-century Mechanical Turk (which proved its intelligence through chess matches) turned out to be simply a man inside a box. Recently, a "hi-tech robot" at a youth science forum in Russia turned out to be pulling the same scam: it, too, was just a man in a robot suit (Roth, 2018). One expert calls it "fake AI" when people are tricked "into believing that what they are seeing is AI when in fact there are human minds behind the scenes" (Wooldridge, 2020, p. 208).

There's a sliding scale of what qualifies as AI these days – it can be thought of as a continuum of capabilities. At the highest level, there is general capability on par with human intelligence; as we go down the scale, applications become more specific and narrowly focused. To categorize these differences, John Searle coined the terms "strong" AI (also known as "general" AI; this AI is capable of general intelligence and performing multiple different tasks at a higher level of abstraction) and "weak" AI (which performs *one* highly specialized AI task with great skill) (Searle, 1980). Currently, there is no strong general AI system, and most experts agree that we are very far from achieving it (Floridi, 2016; Mims, 2017); according to one Stanford computer science professor, "AI has made truly amazing strides in the past decade, but computers still can't exhibit the common sense or the general intelligence of even a five-year-old" (Myers, 2017). All AI programs that currently exist fall into the category of "weak" AI, including those that have grown out of the recent boom in machine learning and neural networks such as machine translation, driverless cars, and game-playing programs. These AI programs are all reasonably effective at carrying out the tasks they have been trained to undertake, but utterly incapable of doing anything else, and they make no claim to human intelligence or consciousness (Wooldridge, 2020, p. 29).

History of AI and Bots

Earlier in Chapter 1, we traced the history of bots in detail from the late 1970s to the present day. Several of the themes we saw in bot evolution are also present in the history of AI as a field. As with bots, AI has been around for nearly as long as computers themselves – indeed, even longer than bots. Many of the earliest developments in AI stem from long before computers. The term *"artificial intelligence"* dates back to 1955, when one of the founders of the field, John McCarthy, used it in a funding proposal for a summer research program at Dartmouth college (Wooldridge, 2020, pp. 37–38). AI's earliest roots are in the 1940s and 1950s, with the foundational development of the *perceptron model*. Inspired by previous research in the 1940s, Professor Frank Rosenblatt developed the perceptron model in the 1950s (McCullough & Pitts, 1943; Rosenblatt, 1958). The model is based on the neuron – the building block of the human brain. At a basic level, the neuron works by receiving analog neural signals as input and transmitting the message to nearby neurons, which in turn repeat the process. Neurons help transmit signals in the brain by working together. The goal of the perceptron was to enable a computer to "learn" on the fly through pattern recognition – to take in information it received and act on it, improving or changing its performance in response (Alpaydin, 2016, pp. 86–87). The Navy claimed the perceptron would be the first non-living machine "capable of receiving, recognizing and identifying its surroundings without any human training or control" (*New York Times*, 1958), and indeed, the perceptron was able to successfully "teach" a computer how to distinguish between left and right – which may sound trivial today, but was in fact an enormous breakthrough. The perceptron is, in fact, the primary basis for the wave of AI progress and enthusiasm that has taken place since 2010.

The task of helping machines learn to change and improve their performance without explicit instruction at each step is a subfield of AI known as *machine learning*. Standard computer programs are a pre-defined series of instructions that direct computers through a pre-defined task – a detailed, step-by-step recipe for how to perform those tasks and process any information it gathers as it does so. In contrast, machine learning programs are iterative, allowing a computer to alter its performance based on what it has already seen in a limited set of previous observations, which are known as *training data*.

The perceptron was one of the first successful implementations of machine learning, and it founded a machine learning approach that has driven many of the past decade's AI breakthroughs. When multiple perceptrons are used together, they form a *multilayer perceptron*, known today as a *neural network*. Neural networks (also known by the name *deep learning*) are behind many of the most impressive recent improvements in AI: they have improved machine translation, helped doctors spot X-ray abnormalities that are imperceptible to the human eye, and enabled the advent of self-driving cars, to name just a few (Wooldridge, 2020, p. 115). As the Cornell Chronicle put it, Rosenblatt's "Perceptron paved the way for AI – 60 years too soon" (Lefkowitz, 2019).

What Limits the Progress of AI?

If the basic theory behind the perceptron was around as early as the 1940s, why did it take more than half a century for neural networks to emerge and drive the modern AI revolution? After all, in the 1950s and 1960s, the new field was frequently the subject of grandiose, sweeping claims about immanent breakthroughs. In 1965, one of the field's founding professors, Herbert Simon, predicted that "within twenty years machines will be capable of doing any work a man can do," and Marvin Minsky, another early pioneer in the field, thought it likely that "within a generation the problem of creating 'artificial intelligence' will be substantially solved"

(Leonard, 1997, p. 32). In 1956, most of Minsky's colleagues at the first AI conference agreed with him (Isaacson, 2014, p. 468).

The reason it took so long to get where we are is that progress in AI has been notoriously uneven and unpredictable. Several key factors have acted as catalysts or bottlenecks for AI progress. One of these is the pace of research and innovation; it takes time to discover the principles and technologies that will allow AI to advance. Perhaps an equally important bottleneck has been computational power, which has long limited the progress of AI as a field. The computational resources required to develop, train, and run deep learning models have only arrived in the past ten years.

Computing power is simply the number of calculations that a computer can carry out per second. The more calculations a computer can complete in a given timespan, the faster it can process information, and the more information it can handle overall. Since the 1960s, computing power has roughly doubled every two years, following a trend known as Moore's law. Computing power has increased as the computing industry has prioritized developing ways to fit more transistors (the things that actually pass the electronic signals that encode the information the computer needs) on the surface of a computer chip. In other words, Moore's law was not an immutable law like that of conservation of momentum; it was a goal that the computer hardware industry worked to fulfill for decades on end (*Economist*, 2016). Experts knew from the early days of the perceptron that the computational resources required to train and implement neural networks simply didn't exist. It was not until 2010, when computational power had substantially increased, and the arrival of graphical processing units (GPUs) and parallel processing had changed the face of modern computing, that computers had the physical capability to store and process the vast amounts of training data. Almost immediately, the availability of this hardware produced significant advances in several AI subfields, such as computer vision and machine translation (Hwang, 2018).

Social factors, too, have hampered AI progress. Social attitudes both in- and outside the field have influenced the rate of progress. Since the field's inception, enthusiasm for AI has waxed and waned. Periods of low enthusiasm for AI research are called *AI Winters* (Markoff, 2015). During boom periods, there are jumps in progress; although the consensus on what approach to AI holds the most promise for the future tends to change, each of these boom periods has added valuable insights and helped progress the field as a whole. The first era of optimism about AI, from the 1950s to the early 1970s, was characterized by an interest in symbolic logical representations. Subsequent waves of AI enthusiasm have emphasized knowledge representation and rule-based approaches (1980s), behavioralist and agent-based approaches (1990s), and finally deep learning and neural networks (roughly 2014 to the present) (Wooldridge, 2020, p. 6). Social attitudes thus influence which subfields and approaches receive attention and investment, and these attitudes determine which subfields progress. For most of AI history, neural networks were not a popular stream of research in the field. As one journalist put it, "computer scientists saw [neural networks] as vaguely disreputable, even mystical" (Lewis-Kraus, 2016).

Finally, the progress of AI research has been most importantly determined by funding. AI is expensive. Without buy-in from funders with deep pockets, it is hard for the field to achieve new breakthroughs. The end of the first AI boom came around the end of the 1960s, when agencies that had been funding AI research in the US and UK commissioned two reports to evaluate the state of progress in AI and certain subfields, such as machine translation. Both reports were critical of AI progress, and this severely limited financial investment in the field. According to the UK's

Lighthill report and the US Automatic Language Processing Advisory Committee (ALPAC) Report, the field had achieved very little after years of funding; this reduced or cut off the flow of money to academics and experts conducting research and driving innovation (Lighthill, 1972; Pierce & Carroll, 1966). Of course, research funding is crucial in any academic discipline, but experts in the AI field highlight the particular impact of these reports, which ushered in the first AI Winter in the early 1970s (Hutchins, 2003; Poibeau, 2017; Wooldridge, 2020, pp. 61–62).

Agent-Based AI, the Semantic Web and Machine Learning

AI is a rich interdisciplinary field with vast and diverse applications. In this chapter, we zero in on the aspects of the field that have most directly impacted bots. Two particular developments have had an outsize impact for bots: the development of the agent-based AI paradigm in the 1990s, and advances in machine learning in the 2010s.

The 1990s saw the third AI boom since the field's inception in the 1950s. This stream of research brought with it a new emphasis on AI programs as "agents," or computational actors, immersed in a particular environment, that were capable of carrying out specialized tasks on behalf of users. Agents were conceived as autonomous programs capable of socially interacting with other users and agents in order to accomplish their pre-defined tasks.

The vision of autonomous agents as the central feature of human–computer interaction is at the heart of Tim Berners-Lee's idealistic vision of the Semantic Web, introduced in the previous chapter. Berners-Lee's goal (one that is still shared by many technologists today) was to automate routine tasks in order to give humans more free time for meaningful pursuits. Technologically speaking, the Semantic Web is at its core a machine-interpretable extension of the World Wide

Web in which agents (or bots) are able to carry out tasks for their hosts (Berners-Lee, 1998). We'll explore this idea more deeply in the conclusion when we examine the future of bots; right now, it's enough to remember that this agent-centric vision of the future is closely intertwined with the idea of agent-based AI and bots.

The idea that agents could be autonomous actors that allowed humans to connect with computers was a big shift, moving away from the robotics conception of a hardware-based agent and toward a more software-oriented one – something closer to what we now call a bot. Agents would be able to fetch and process emails, surf the web, and work with humans via an agent-based interface (Wooldridge, 2020, pp. 96–99), streamlining human workflows and interactions by taking care of monotonous tasks like scheduling appointments (Maes, 1994). These were new conceptions of the capabilities and purpose of bots. The computing power necessary to bring these visions to life – and the machine learning techniques that enabled them to work autonomously – wouldn't come for another two decades, but the ethos of agent-based AI that emerged in the 1990s was foundational for our modern AI assistants like Amazon's Alexa, Apple's Siri, Google Home, and Microsoft's Cortana (Maes, 1994; Wooldridge, 2020, p. 98).

The 1990s breakthrough in thinking about autonomous agents needed one more element to be realized – a development that also required the increases in data storage and computing power of the 2010s. This development was machine learning, an AI subdiscipline concerned with teaching machines how to learn and recognize patterns from a limited set of inputs (Hwang, 2018), which most directly helped produce today's bots and AI. Indeed, what today the press and public call AI is, in nearly all cases, actually a form of machine learning. Some funders and practitioners even take the terms as synonymous for now – in interview with two AI experts, one venture capitalist referred to AI and deep learning (a form of machine learning) as "completely interchangeable" (Elish & Hwang, 2016).

Machine learning comes in two main forms, supervised and unsupervised. The goal of supervised learning is to "train" a computer with *labeled* examples of patterns that it is supposed to recognize in the wild. Supervised learning is often used for classification tasks – determining whether an input example belongs to a certain category (for example, whether a given Twitter account is a bot or not). At the most basic level, supervised machine learning algorithm tells you whether or not a given input matches a pre-defined category based on the data it has seen before (Alpaydin, 2016, pp. 38–54). When a supervised machine learning model sifts through training data it examines thousands, or even millions, of examples of labeled data and then learns which *features* of each instance of data are most *predictive* of belonging to a particular category, then outputs its best guess about whether a given input example belongs to that category.

A concrete example of this may be useful. One form of supervised learning is a language model – an algorithm that tells you what language a given sentence is written in. Say we are looking for sentences in French. We could train a computer on 2,000 sentences, 1,000 in French (labeled as "French") and 1,000 in other languages (labeled as "not French"). From these examples, the computer would extract certain features that are predictive of a sentence being written in French – perhaps the presence of accented characters like *é*, *è*, or *à*, or the appearance of the words *un*, *une*, *le*, and *la*. This process would produce an extremely basic classifier that could tell us whether any given sentence is written in French. This model would work at a very basic level.

In contrast, with *unsupervised machine learning*, the data given to the computer is not labeled; it is simply fed into the computer, which learns whatever associations it can from the examples, then "clusters" them according to similarities it identifies. For example, neural networks can extract common patterns from images, and they can therefore "recognize" whether a panda bear is present in a photograph. The computer has no understanding of what a panda actually is, but using unsupervised learning, it can detect that a set of panda photos have *something* in common in the form of digital signatures (colors, outlines, etc.), and it can use those features to judge whether other photos contain pandas. It is hard to overstate the impact of unsupervised learning, especially deep learning/neural networks, on AI progress in the past decade.

The basic difference between these two forms of machine learning is that in *supervised* learning, the computer knows what it is looking for – the data it learns from are *labeled* (by human experts) to give the computer the information it needs. In *unsupervised* learning, the computer is given free rein to find whatever patterns it can in the examples provided to it, with no pre-defined goal. For high-quality, robust results, both supervised and unsupervised machine learning require good training data: it should be *representative, diverse, high-quality* – likely to reflect what the computer encounters in the wild – and should be large enough for the computer to find significant patterns in the data points.

How Bots Use AI

As we've seen, AI is an interdisciplinary field with extremely broad and diverse applications. Exploring all the ways that bots use AI is a topic that could rightfully deserve its own book. Here, we will focus on two main AI applications that are central to bots as we've explored them in this book: bot detection (bots identifying other bots) and processing human language (a field known as Natural Language Processing, or NLP).

Bot detection

Perhaps somewhat paradoxically, bots are increasingly being used for the task of catching other (malicious) bots, and bot detection has begun to make use of AI techniques. Several bot-detecting bots are active on Twitter, such as botcheck.me and Bot Sentinel. Many of these tools use machine learning to detect other bots on the platform and then post tweets about what they have found (BotSentinel.com, 2020).

The use of bots for bot detection arguably began with the arrival of CAPTCHAs in the 1990s. CAPTCHA stands for "Completely Automated Public Turing test to tell Computers and Humans Apart." These are the frequent (and sometimes annoying) tests that internet users frequently have to pass in order to access services online – tasks that are trivial for humans (e.g. type the word you see here, choose all the photos with fire hydrants in them, etc.), but difficult or impossible for bots. As bots have multiplied, so have CAPTCHA tests; in 2010, Google was already serving up to 15,000 CAPTCHAs a second on its properties (Tarnoff & Weigel, 2020, p. 84). Today, humans solve over a billion CAPTCHAs per day (*Live Bitcoin News*, 2018). They are so ubiquitous that comedian John Mulaney complained in 2020 that "you spend most of your day telling a robot you're not a robot."

CAPTCHAs are a microcosm of the bot-detection world at large. In the 1990s, CAPTCHAs were trivial, mostly consisted of typing a small number of clear letters or numbers visible in an image. As bots grew more advanced, they were able to overcome these tests, and CAPTCHA designers innovated in response, adding in colors and distorting letters to prevent bots from successfully reading the images using optical character recognition (OCR) software (Burling, 2012; Dzieza, 2019). This is another example of "arms race" between bot builders and bot detectors we alluded to in Chapter 3: the advantage seesaws between one side and the other, alternating as each side innovates to defeat the other (Cresci et al., 2017). Today's CAPTCHAs now involve multiple stages and image-based tests. Who knows how bots will learn to evade these, and what CAPTCHA designers will do in response.

CAPTCHAs are a very simple example of bot detection. Far more advanced and involved techniques are used to detect social bots on social media. In the early 2010s, machine learning-based bot detectors frequently used supervised learning techniques to classify individual accounts as being a "bot or not" by feeding large numbers of accounts labeled "bot" or "human" to an algorithm, which then used this data as a basis for future predictions. This approach arguably worked well enough for a time, but it was subject to several well-known problems. One is the "ground truth problem" – the bot and human "labels" used in training data are human judgments, and current evidence suggests that humans are not particularly good at these assessments (Edwards et al., 2014; Subrahmanian et al., 2016). Supervised techniques from the early part of the decade also focused on individual accounts rather than networks. (It was in response to these supervised learning bot detection schemes that the cyborgs (discussed in Chapter 2) arose. Cyborgs confuse the categorization algorithm: they have some traits of fully automated accounts and some traits of real human accounts, so they are very difficult to identify as bots.)

To address these shortcomings, bot detection tools began to use unsupervised machine learning techniques such as neural networks after 2012, when deep learning became truly viable. Today, there are roughly as many unsupervised bot detection tools as supervised. Whichever approach is taken, machine learning and artificial intelligence lie at the core of modern-day bot detection. The most recent techniques involve incorporating a machine learning technique known as Generative Adversarial Networks (GANs) and network analysis techniques to identify automated accounts (Cresci, 2020).

Chatbots and Natural Language Processing (NLP)

One of the most important ways that bots use AI is to understand and produce human language, or "natural language" as it is known in computer science. The bots that interact with humans using natural language are chatbots, which we have discussed in detail in previous chapters.

Under the hood, chatbots can take different approaches to engage in conversation with humans and, as we have seen in previous chapters, not all of them use AI techniques. The techniques used by non-AI bots tend to either be rule-based, which rely on carefully stipulated rules for how to process conversational inputs, or corpus-based, which use vast amounts of data (known as "linguistic corpora") as a reservoir of examples that craft how a bot responds to an utterance (Jurafsky & Martin, 2018). Two bots we have met already, ELIZA and Eugene Goostman, both used the former approach of pre-defined, rule-based heuristics to simulate human conversation.

Non-AI chatbots

Most non-AI chatbots use rule-based techniques. The most basic chatbots use pattern matching, keywords, and canned phrases to simulate conversation with humans. Bots like these are typically used in extremely narrow and constrained contexts, such as customer service – and environments where the bot is likely to encounter only a small set of utterances.

At the most basic level, a chatbot simply spits out preformulated sentences regardless of user input. Bots like these include the @everyword bot, which tweets every word of the English language from a dictionary but does not interact with other users on Twitter (Dubbin, 2013). The next step up from this most primitive type is a chatbot that has basic input processing: it searches for keywords and patterns in user input and responds to each keyword with preformulated responses. Think of a customer service bot that asks what it can help you with, but simply waits for you to mention the name of a product it provides support for so it can direct you to a webpage about that product. You can spend all day in an unproductive loop with these bots because they don't know what to say unless you mention the particular product name they're looking for in all of your dialogue.

A slightly more advanced form of chatbot combines input processing with memory. ELIZA is the canonical example of this category of chatbot. Like simpler chatbots, ELIZA used pattern matching, keywords, and set phrases within the narrow context of a self-help conversation to simulate conversation, but one of its more innovative functionalities – one that improved its simulation of human conversation – was its ability to remember earlier elements of the conversation and ask questions about them (Jurafsky & Martin, 2020). As we learned earlier, ELIZA strategically changed the topic when it encountered an unforeseen sentence for which it had no response. When this happened, ELIZA changed to a topic encountered earlier in the conversation. This was a subtle way to avoid veering into conversation that was too advanced for the bot, while also making it seem like an attentive listener. While ELIZA was influential enough to stun many of its conversational partners and inspire *"the ELIZA effect,"* it cannot be said to have used AI in any real sense of the term. For decades, however, ELIZA remained the most impressive chatbot in existence, and its basic approach was a model for many important bot successors such as the online gaming MUDbots in the 1980s and 1990s, such as A.L.I.C.E. (a natural language chatterbot that has won the Loebner Prize for passing the Turing test three times), and Albert One (another chatterbot using NLP that twice won the Loebner Prize) (Deryugina, 2010).

Corpus-based chatbots and fuzzy logic

In the past two decades, as data became easier and cheaper to store and computing power increased, more computationally expensive, statistical pattern-matching techniques emerged. These bots gleaned patterns from vast troves of language data (linguistic corpora). One of the first chatbots to enhance its performance with these statistical techniques was Rollo Carpenter's Cleverbot. Like other ELIZA-style bots, Cleverbot uses keyword recognition, pattern matching, and remembers conversation context. However, it has an additional conversational database that it consults in real time to improve its conversational performance. Since coming online in 1997, Cleverbot has had tens of millions of conversations with humans on its open web interface. Cleverbot saves dialogue from these conversations in a database and uses them as a reference for future conversations. (Existor, 2014; Wolchover, 2011).

At the core of Cleverbot's functionality is a technique known as fuzzy matching. Fuzzy matching is a form of "fuzzy logic," a strategy that computers use to deal with the ambiguity and uncertainty of human language (Alpaydin, 2016, p. 51; Zadeh, 1965). When Cleverbot encounters an utterance that does not match a keyword or pattern it has been programmed to respond to, it scans its linguistic database of over 170 million lines of previous dialogue and finds an answer that seems most natural, based on past responses that it has given or that humans have typed. The term "fuzzy" comes from the fact that Cleverbot is using an *approximate* match to determine the best response. While this approach does not always produce an appropriate answer, it gives the computer a better shot at simulating human conversation than not answering at all or answering with a clearly inappropriate canned response.

AI-based chatbots

However, heuristics and pattern matching can only take a bot so far. The most impressive recent chatbots tend to incorporate AI techniques. In addition to AI techniques, AI-based chatbots can and often do use both rule-based and corpus-based techniques to enhance their performance in conversation.

They also use various statistical techniques to increase the accuracy and appropriateness of their responses. As we know, data can be mined to learn associations and patterns, and the more data you have for a computer to learn from, the better it will be at performing the target task. When data is analyzed using probability techniques (such as Bayesian methods and Markov Chains), it helps AI and NLP applications to better understand and generate natural language, particularly in dealing with the ambiguity and uncertainty they encounter while parsing human language. Many of the most advanced chatbots of today analyze massive troves of language data online to learn word associations. These bots use statistical methods known as Markov Chains – which, as we learned in Chapter 1, are a technique used by one of the most impressive Usenet bots to produce realistic posts in the 1990s. These statistical analysis bots work by computing what words are most likely to follow other words based on previously collected language examples. The more data these programs have to rely on, the more natural and human-like their speech is likely to be. These techniques underlie the most impressive chatbots of the current generation.

Conversational interfaces and AI assistant chatbots

One of the most-used types of chatbots today is the conversational AI assistant. These chatbots have become commonplace in the last five years, and today, almost everyone reading this will recognize Apple's Siri, Amazon's Alexa, Microsoft's Cortana, and Google Home. Similar smart speakers with internet assistants are also being produced by Chinese tech companies for the Chinese market (Prist, 2019).

These systems generally use a conversational user interface (CUI) to receive audio input from users – core functionalities that depend on AI. Computers generally convert spoken audio input to text using machine learning techniques known as Automatic Speech Recognition (ASR) before they start to parse the sentence and try to understand its meaning.

Currently, conversational AI assistants are incapable of open-ended conversation. To process human language, bots need real-world knowledge to understand the meanings of words and the relationships between them. For instance, when a person hears the sentence "I dropped the steel ball on the glass table and it shattered," they immediately understand that "it" refers to the glass table. This is obvious to humans, who know that glass is more likely to shatter than steel (Hall, 2019). For a computer to understand what "it" refers to, they must make these same connections; because they have no material experience of the world, this requires AI designers to embed meaning in the system using a form of *knowledge representation*, teaching the machines the basic real-world knowledge they need to process language. This is typically done using knowledge graphs – machine-readable networks that encode information about things in the world and relationships between them.

Obviously, it's impossible to diagram all of the things in the world and the relationships between them. Nevertheless, Google's Knowledge Graph aims to do just this, and it has diagrammed over 500 billion facts about five billion entities. For the time being, though, it is much more feasible to build smaller-scale representations of specific domains, limiting the kinds of inferences the AI must make to properly understand commands and assist humans

(Sullivan, 2020). Knowledge representations in modern AI assistants therefore tend to be task-based – they can play music, adjust lights or temperature within a home, or help to search for information on the web, because each of these specific tasks falls into a small domain in which only a small number of keywords and relationships, embedded only with their task-specific meanings, are needed to carry out the user's instructions.

While much of the technology that AI assistants rely on to work was developed only relatively recently (such as cloud computing and ASR algorithms), the knowledge representation framework that they use to parse meaning from spoken sentences dates back to the late 1970s. The 1977 GUS framework is a relatively simple way of representing meaning for a given task that works using *frame semantics* (Bobrow et al., 1977). Essentially, GUS breaks down a task into the small number of units of meaning necessary to carry out that task. These units are known as *slots*, and once the computer fills these slots, it can carry out the task for the user. For instance, if you are booking a flight, a computer would need to know your departure city, your destination city, and your desired travel dates. All of the pre-defined questions it asks you are geared toward filling these semantic slots. After all the slots are filled, the assistant can carry out the action.

This frame-based infrastructure underlies nearly all popular AI assistants today. The process of building frames that are relevant to a given task is known as building a *domain ontology*. Essentially, this is a form of knowledge representation that defines the nouns and relationships that are necessary for the computer to carry out a task like booking your flight (Jurafsky & Martin, 2020). Conversational AI assistants are in a relatively early stage of development. For now – as regular users of these AI assistants are all too aware – their understanding of human language is extremely limited.

Open-domain chatbots

Because the conversational AI assistants discussed above can only operate within a very limited domain of conversation, we call them closed-domain chatbots. The holy grail of chatbots is an open-domain bot – one capable of human-level diversity of conversation that is not confined to a task-specific domain. Human conversations are unstructured, can move from topic to topic, and last for varying lengths of time. Recently, data-driven techniques that train text-based chatbots on billions of words have brought us one tiny step closer to this goal (Jurafsky & Martin, 2020; Serban et al., 2017). For example, Google's Meena bot, trained on 341 GB of text from online social media conversations, achieved impressive performance as one of the first text-based chatbots trained on these massive amounts of data (Adiwardana et al., 2020; Adiwardana & Luong, 2020). Perhaps the most impressive chatbots trained on huge corpora are the generative pretrained transformer (GPT) chatbots. As of this writing, GPT-3 is the third and latest generation chatbot in the GPT series. GPT-3 was trained on vast amounts of data – nearly 45 TB of text data, much more than any previous chatbot, including Meena – and uses both unsupervised and supervised machine learning techniques to learn how to put together sentences in a way that seems human (T. B. Brown et al., 2020). GPT-3 only requires a small number of examples to mimic effectively what has been given to it. For example, if you give GPT a poem, it will spit back poems mimicking the style of the examples you gave it. Users define the tone and register of what they want GPT-3 to mimic with a small number of examples they feed it, and then the bot starts producing similar content. In 2020, the bot generated convincing news articles, blog posts, and even computer code (GPT-3, 2020; Metz, 2020; *Economist*, 2020). Currently, GPT-3 is the state-of-the-art in chatbots, and it is a significant advancement toward an open-domain chatbot that can effectively mimic human conversation.

Conclusion

As we've seen, AI is helping to transform what bots are capable of doing, particularly in the areas of NLP and bot detection. There is still much left undone, and many questions on the horizon. As we saw with the example of Tay in Chapter 4, human inputs to AI systems can result in technological and social failures. Importantly, these inputs come not only from bot designers themselves as they write the code underpinning the bots they deploy, but also from users as they interact with AI-powered bots who learn from them. The future of bots and AI is still indistinct, but there are several important areas likely to spur new stages of bot evolution. We'll return to a deeper discussion of these areas and the very important ethical concerns they raise for our final chapter, The Future of Bots.

6

Theorizing the Bot

In early 2015 the police knocked on Jeffry van der Goot's door. The cops told Jeffry, who is non-binary and uses the pronouns they/them, that they were under investigation: an account linked to their name had been making death threats on Twitter (Hern, 2015). The account, @jeffrybooks, tweeted a message saying: "I seriously want to kill people" and mentioned an upcoming fashion convention in Amsterdam. The police were concerned. Could this be a credible threat aimed at people attending the event? Was van der Goot planning something?

Not only did van der Goot have no nefarious or violent intentions, they didn't even write the tweet. The account in question was run by a bot that Jeffry had built. The bot, named Jeff_ebooks, was designed to randomly create and share sentences or phrases (Hill, 2015). It was powered by a Markov Chain generator, a basic algorithm used to create somewhat realistic sounding posts by randomly drawing from a specific, pre-programmed body of text. In this case, it was set to randomly splice in words from Jeffry's own (human-run) personal Twitter account. Jeffry had let the bot loose, and it had gotten into hot water. To make matters more confusing, Jeff_ebooks made the death threat in a conversation with another Twitter bot account: the two went back and forth until eventually, Jeff_ebooks shared its homicidal tweet. It was bot-on-bot violence.

According to the police, Jeffry was liable for the actions of their Twitter account, but ultimately, they simply forced Jeffry to delete the account. The situation left Jeffry feeling shaken.

"Being interviewed by detectives is incredibly stressful, terrifying and intimidating," they told the *Guardian* (Hern, 2015). While van der Goot apologized, they made it clear that they weren't really sure they were to blame: the bot was randomly putting together words to form coherent sentences. Yes, Jeffry launched the bot, but they didn't expect it to do what it did. And Jeffry's code was actually based upon that of another user, Wxcafe, who also shared a public apology and expressed surprise at what had transpired. So, questions of responsibility or culpability were complex. Once launched, the bot was operating independently on the social media platform, and it had behaved in ways that its creator didn't expect.

The curious case of Jeff_ebooks is one example among many of bots engaging in unpredictable behavior. A similar incident took place in Switzerland, with a bot-driven art exhibit. The bot, known as the Random Darknet Shopper, was built to use Bitcoin to make arbitrary purchases on the Dark Web. Swiss police caught the bot buying ecstasy and other illicit and illegal products (Kasperkevic, 2015). Of course, the bot was built to "explore" this shadowy layer of the internet by buying things there, and the Dark Web is hidden for a reason; most of the activity there is illicit in some way. Perhaps its creators should have expected such an outcome. But both Jeff_ebooks and the Random Darknet Shopper bring up important questions relating to the complex role bots play in life online.

Who is responsible for the actions of Jeff_ebooks and Random Darknet Shopper? This question raises other questions about bots as participants in social relationships, both with those who create them and those who use or encounter them. As we have discussed several times in previous chapters, bots reflect their creators' values; how, then, can they perform unexpected or unpredicted actions? More broadly, these stories ask us to consider bots' sociocultural role on the web, both on and off social media. Bots are definitionally autonomous objects, but perhaps they can also drive sociality; perhaps, as bots encoded to exercise machine learning discover and use information from the broader online world, they can affect our human social norms, rules, or connections. But how can bots, made up of layers of code, change human culture?

This chapter explores these questions, giving an overview of academic theories that speak to the role of bots in our world – what we might think of as philosophies of the bot. This discussion is aimed at scholars of the social sciences and humanities who want to gain a cursory understanding of the current debates around bots. This chapter, like this book, is not an exhaustive dive into the literature we sketch out here. In fact, one could dedicate an entire career to studying and advancing any one of the theories presented below. So, with this in mind, we offer short, approachable, explanations of bot theories and encourage those interested in particular points to delve deeper. We foreground these explanations with this book's overarching argument – bots are widespread and crucial to the functioning of our digitally dependent modern world. With this in mind, it is very important to explore these automated tools theoretically in order to address the question: what ideas and principles ought to guide our understandings of bots?

Some of the theories in this chapter consider the "lives" of bots. Others suggest that bots have unique connective power that could be leveraged to connect separate cultural, professional, or political groups, stitching them together like patches in a quilt to help them realize their societal or civic potential. Still others address the imaginary of the bot and its intelligence: powered by sophisticated AI or machine learning, bots sometimes seem to function as "intelligent" actors, and other times they seem simply procedural or rote. How can we reconcile these roles? Meanwhile, scholars including Bucher (Bucher, 2014) explore the ways in which social media bots complicate notions of "personas" via their para-social relationships with people as well as the intricacies of how humans and automated machines communicate (Guzman & Lewis, 2020).

To shed light on related work, we first turn to scholarship in science and technology studies, media studies, information science, communication, and sociology, examining theories that broadly examine the social, informative, and communicative roles played by non-human actors and technology. Here, we focus on Suchman's (2006) concept of situated action, the work of Latour and others (2007) on actor network theory, and Nardi's (1995) take on activity theory. We detail the general premises of these theories and discuss how they apply to bots. We also discuss contemporary theories that specifically focus on the interactions between social media bots and humans, including Neff and Nagy's (2016) idea of bot and human symbiosis, Guilbeault's (2016) overview of bot ecology, and Woolley's conception of manufactured consensus (2018). We also investigate how bots operate as proxies of their creators (Woolley, Shorey, & Howard, 2018) – related but separate to the people that build them, while, in many cases, being open to inputs from the external world online.

Next, we turn to theories of bots' infrastructural roles – not just as technological infrastructure but as social infrastructure. We build on the conceptualizations detailed above regarding the relationships between human and automated actors online to discuss how bots can serve as social scaffolding or civic prostheses – how they might be used to help or harm community connections and democratic engagement. We then explore theories of bots' more technological roles as invisible organizers and laborers online. These theories include Geiger's (2014; 2018) work on Wikipedia bots, Hepp's (2020) discussion of "communicative" bots, and Summers and Punzalan's (2017) analysis of archival bots. We conclude with a discussion about the theoretical edges of bot scholarship: where does this area of study seem to be going and where is there more work to be done?

Theorizing Human–Computer Interaction and Human–Machine Communication

To consider the socio-cultural role of bots, we must first ask a broader question: how can a non-human "thing," "tool," or "artifact" be meaningfully involved in society? Can something that is non-sentient and non-living be said to generate social or cultural change, or is it simply doing what it is designed or pre-programmed (quite literally, in the case of bots) to do? If "things" can, in fact, effect social change, we must imagine *how* they do so, and we must consider how much of their effect is in fact caused by their human creators – the problem that plagued the programmers of Jeff_ebooks and Random Darknet Shopper. In other words, to understand whether bots are truly social actors, we must first decide whether they have power and agency.

These questions are necessarily interdisciplinary, for they touch on the relation of the scientific (digital hardware and software) to the social (the humans that design the technology and the social worlds in which these devices operate). Therefore, work in many fields has sought to address them: computer and information sciences, anthropology, sociology, and other fields within the social sciences and humanities have all contributed to answering these questions. Now, there are whole fields and subfields that seek these answers: fields of science and technology studies (or science, technology and society studies – STS) and human–computer interaction (HCI) and the subfield of human–machine communication (HMC).

Overview of the Literature

Winner (1980) provides an early discussion on the politics of technological artifacts. He argues that such tools do, in fact, maintain authority and exercise control – they can discriminate, influence, and dictate. Preece et al. (1994)

present an overarching explanation of HCI, including and beyond power dynamics, and offer a starting point for understanding the exchange between humans and the digital world. But the outcomes of interactions between humans and computers are often complex and hard to predict, and Schneiderman and Plaisant (2009, pp. 423–434) argue that new technology designs or software can produce unforeseen social and individual implications.

Suchman (2006) explains how these unforeseen consequences are possible, He argues that builders cannot and do not plan for every possible outcome when they construct objects. Engineers' actions are situated – contextual and often ad hoc, based on unexamined assumptions grounded in their memories of space and place, tacit knowledge, situational awareness, and beliefs based upon experience. The tools they create (especially, says Suchman, the digital or automated ones) bring these hidden assumptions about the world to the forefront. For example, when an engineer has not been the subject of hate speech themselves, they may make a chatbot that draws from a large corpus of non-preselected text but is not pre-programmed to avoid certain words or phrases. Like Tay, or like Jeffry_ebooks, these bots reflect their programmers' somewhat insular or naive experience of the world, and may (in fact, almost certainly will) end up saying something problematic, hurtful, or harmful.

Plans, then, are necessarily incomplete and must be open to change. We must constantly be ready to step in and fix divergent behavior from computational systems, especially from AI systems. This means that building and launching thoughtful digital technology is a process of foresight and planning, yes, but also one of attentiveness, maintenance, and care. Dourish (2004) calls this process of engaged engineering and design "embodied interaction" and argues that this should be our mode of operation: humility and openness to revision rather than ideas about technology as universal, abstract, and fully rational.

These premises set the stage for other theorizations of human–computer interaction and human–machine communication. They invited new questions: If digital tools have politics, and if our relationship with them is dictated as much by surprises as by planned actions, then what are the specifics of how these "things" act and react in the broader world – in social networks, in cultural frameworks and, more simply, in their interactions with both disembodied code and people on the web? Nardi (1995) offers the solution of activity theory, a set of principles for understanding "practice," which grew out of Soviet psychological research in the early twentieth century. She presents it as a remedy for STS and HCI scholars "struggl[ing] to understand and describe 'context,' 'situation,' 'practice'"(p. 4) in the face of preconceived academic notions about scientific objectivity and positivist purity – about the problem of contextualizing scientific or engineering outcomes within the context of the planning that produced them. Researchers have begun to accept that human–machine relationships are situational, rather than mechanical or pre-planned, but Nardi's activity theory goes further; it offers grounding concepts and terminology – an entire theory of things that would otherwise be interpreted as of-the-moment reactions. She uses this theory to suggest that HCI can benefit from both rigorous science *and* participatory design – the latter of which gives primacy to socially responsible science, technology, engineering, and mathematics (STEM) work (p. 7). Meanwhile, scholars of human machine communication have asked similar questions vis-à-vis the fields of communication and media studies (Oberquelle et al., 1983). They explore the complexities of various digital technologies, including bots, information spreading capabilities alongside and in comparison with human and semi-human actors (Guzman, 2018).

Callon (1986), Akrich (1987), Law and Hassard (1999), Latour (2007), and others extend ideas about how tools, technologies, and "things" operate alongside people by exploring them as networks. They call this conceptualization actor network theory (ANT). Their idea of "the network" speaks to the interconnected communities or systems within which a group or individual "actor" operates. Networks are defined by the relationships they comprise between individuals and items, from computers in digital ecosystems to plants and animals in the natural world. Law describes ANT as "a disparate family of material-semiotic tools, sensibilities, and methods of analysis that treat everything in the social and natural worlds as a continuously generated effect of the webs of relations within which they are located" (B. S. Turner, 2009). The focus on both material (objects) and semiotic (ideas or symbols) suggests that relationships, and the networks in which they exist, are more than just connections between two things (whether people, bots, or dogs) but involve loaded conceptualizations of those things. For instance, a social bot, the code that orders the bot's behavior,[1] and a particular group's understanding of that social bot all add to social context. Social context is dictated by more than *just* human interactions or perceptions but also the objects they interact with – the objects of human perception. The most controversial element of this theory – and also the element potentially most relevant to theorizing the social role of bots – is ANT's assertion that all manner of nonhumans – and specifically digital objects – are actually actors (Latour, 2011). They can enact change within a network, and they can drive sociality. This means that to understand collective behaviors, we must contextualize all interactions – including those between humans and technological objects – within this multi-faceted network of things, ideas, and people (Kono, (2013).

As this overview of foundational scholarship into the human–object relationship has shown, many theorists believe that objects such as bots have a role in the sociocultural world: they effect and are part of relationships, values, norms, and beliefs. As Winner (1980) pointed out more than four decades ago, artifacts (or things/objects) are imbued with meaning and intentions, and this, along with their ability to operate in complex human–machine systems, gives them power. Nardi showed us that that power is contextual or situated, and that it can produce unexpected consequences. We can understand unexpected or unplanned-for results by interrogating the practices or activities that surround them, rather than treating technologies and technical processes as somehow pre-ordained via positivist notions of objectivity and parsimony. Finally, ANT showed us that the networks in which humans operate are situated among and include all manner of objects (what Winner called artifacts) and ideas.

The Human–Bot Relationship

The complex socio-cultural impact of technology grounds questions about the human–bot relationship. Even for those who disagree with the positions enumerated above, there is no question that bots necessarily have a relationship to the human. Bots are, after all, built by humans, and they are often built in the human image. Social bots, in particular, are regularly built to mimic the behaviors of human social media users. Bots programmed with machine learning can even learn from other people, as well as the creations of other people, such as their bots. This learning means that their functions or "personalities" change – they could even be said to be crowd-sourced by the entire network in which the bot exists. But bots could not exist without the people who build them. So, bots are certainly human creations. But are they simply products of their builders, or are they extensions of their builders? According to bot theory, both of these things are true. Because many bots display situational behavior, and because some are built to learn from the eco-systems within which they operate, some scholars (Abokhodair et al., 2015) suggest they are automated social actors (ASAs):

The level of sophistication and the roles that a given ASA will fill in the social space can vary. An ASA could be relatively simple, like bots that aggregate information from web news and re-present it as a set of tweets in Twitter, or quite sophisticated like a conversational bot that is attempting to pass a Turing test. (p. 840)

According to this understanding, an ASA might be an actor programmed to do "good" or "bad"[2] things on behalf of their creator, but ultimately they are merely another part of the online social space with which we, as humans, must understand and interact.

As is clear from Jeffry's experience and that of the Random Darknet Shopper bot's creators, the theoretical work of Suchman (2006), Nardi (1995), and others is correct: some bots are capable of operating in ways unforeseen even by their creators. How does this extend their social role beyond something that is purely automated? "Automation" speaks to a repetitive, mechanical process. When bots behave unexpectedly, they seem to be operating beyond pure automation. Because of this, many ANT inspired theorists argue that some bots can be seen as complex actors rather than purely rote ones. Bots are not necessarily limited by pre-programmed automated tasks but can effect their own unique versions of change.

For Hegelich and Janetzko (2016), the changes that social bots generate can be attributed to three different bot behaviors: mimicry, window dressing, and reverberation. Through empirical analysis of a Ukrainian political botnet, they conclude that the bots in question were built to have their own political agenda. Their coders construct them to practice mimicry, or "try to hide their bot-identity" (p. 582). They use the tactic of window dressing: working to be interesting to other social media users by promoting popular topics or hashtags. Finally, they reverberate: they echo or reshare others' messages. Hegelich and Janetzko argue that the bots have autonomy from their human "botmasters" and that their behavior is not simply dictated by a "simple deterministic structure of command" (p. 582), they do not speak to the larger socio-cultural questions these assertions raise. What do these behaviors mean about the human–bot connection in this particular case – are they imbued with their creators' political or cultural biases or separate from their designers' social baggage?

Neff and Nagy (2016) seek to answer questions like these. They suggest that bots and their builders (and, more broadly, social bots and the larger social networks within which they operate) have a symbiotic relationship. Using the case of Tay, Microsoft's failed machine learning Twitter bot, they argue that the behavior of social bots is best understood through "symbiotic agency" that is connected to the "imagined affordances" of emerging technology. They point out that other users on social media platforms often ascribe agency and personality to bots like Tay; they imagine that such a bot is autonomous and therefore personify it. But when the bot does something unexpected or unseemly, they immediately place blame upon the bot's designers or other actors involved in "training" the bot's behavior. With Tay, people blamed Microsoft engineers for not pre-programming the bot to avoid hate speech, as well as the human trolls who taught her to spew such vitriol. But Neff and Nagy argue that Tay's agency – and her connection to those who had a hand in her output – is more complicated than that: "The concepts of agency and affordance must evolve if scholars and designers are to move beyond deterministic, bifurcated ways of thinking about agency as separable into technological scaffolding and humanistic action" (p. 4927). We must ask *how* bots operate outside our imagined constructions of their behavior, and look for other socio-technically informed inputs and outputs that we miss if we focus only on the most obvious origins of bot behavior.

Woolley, Shorey, and Howard (2018) pick up these inquiries. After conducting a series of interviews with bot makers in which they asked makers to reflect on the actions of their socially facing bots, they conclude that bots are *proxies* for their creators – both connected to and separate from those who build them. Social bots often contain some of their builders' social baggage, but they also often behave within their ecosystems in unexpected, even shocking, ways. "Bots are more than tools," they argue, "but they are not sentient or independently emotive" (p. 59). Instead, "they reflect the thoughts and emotions of the builder, while also reacting to the networked computational systems in which they operate" (p. 59). Like Nagy and Neff, Woolley et al. argue that scholars must not oversimplify the complex actor-oriented role of bots. Ultimately, they argue that to understand bots' divergent, unique, status as actors, social scientists must compare the effects of social bots to the expectations of their creators.

Because bot behaviors (and especially political bot behaviors) are complex and often controversial, Guilbeault (2016) argues for the development of a hybrid theory of ethics for understanding bots' roles in online life. Social media, he argues, "propel bots into agency" (p. 5004). Changes in the online ecology, showcased on platforms like Facebook and Twitter, mean that bots are now acceptable, and they can therefore interact more effectively with other users. According to Guilbeault, these changes make obsolete the arguments of Kennedy (2009) and Miller (2007), who deny the agency of bots based on analyses of less-bot-friendly internet spaces and earlier versions of social media. Guilbeault suggests that:

> An ecological approach to bots focuses on interface features of networking platforms as targets of intervention and innovation, thereby expanding the scope of bot security. [...] Most important, it opens toward a hybrid ethics, wherein humans and bots act together to solve problems in internet security. (p. 5004)

Here, Guilbeault frames the bot as a potential ally in internet security, and offers a novel definition of bot agency that is tied to bots' integration into online social worlds, which has become increasingly more seamless. Social media now exist in formats more easily trafficked and exploited by bots. For Guilbeault, bots are an integral part of many social networking systems, and they therefore must help to combat adverse manipulation of those systems. For him, bots are therefore meaningful agents (or actors) within these systems. He points to the work of Hwang, Pearce, and Nanis (2012) as concretizing his notion that shifts in the online ecology are changing the role of bots online. According to Hwang et al., "digitization drives botification: the use of technology in the realm of human activity enables the creation of software to act in lieu of humans" (p. 4). So the agency or influence of bots is directly tied not only to the people who build them and interact with them but also to the systems in which they operate.

Do bots need to be intelligent or sentient to affect the worlds in which they operate? The scholars above each answer this with some version of a "no," suggesting that bots can be considered actors simply because of their unique positionality and capabilities in the online sphere, not because of any particular claim to intelligence. In fact, Assenmacher et al. (2020) argue that in general, bots are not as "smart" as some believe. Recent reports on their role in global political communication indicates that most bots operating online, far from being artificially intelligent, actually play support roles; they are designed to provide "modules of automation" rather than to navigate the internet intelligently. Grimme et al. (2017) suggest that social bots have the same shortcomings that preclude them from being judged intelligent, for their interactive capabilities are similarly quite limited in their general use across social media platforms.

So, there is a growing body of work, primarily focusing on social bots, suggesting that bots have some degree of agency online – agency that is simultaneously connected to and separate from people. But what about less social, more infrastructural bots? For instance, can we classify bots that operate on the so-called "back end" of social media platforms or other websites as some form of "actor"? Woolley et al. (2018) argue that the answer is often yes, because these bots are also built to communicate autonomously – only their communication is with other machines rather than directly with people. According to ANT, these bot–bot interactions would be no less valid, no less "social," than bot–human interactions, for connections between objects are equally part of a network as connections between objects and people. The authors note that like social bots, back-end bots can also be programmed to learn from their environments. They also point to the bot builders they interviewed, who suggested that (like social bots), back-end bots often did unexpected things, again because of the unique inputs and outputs of the ecosystems that they inhabited.

The Infrastructural Role of Bots

Most people never think about the back-end bots that serve as the infrastructure of the internet. A lot of us navigate the web without ever realizing that we are constantly interacting with bots. When we do engage with an obvious bot, like a customer-service chatbot, we are unlikely to think of it as a particular kind of interactive bot that is part of a bot-based infrastructure; we usually think of it as simply an automated commercial system. But as you now no doubt realize, bots exist in a variety of capacities online. Ways of understanding these bots, likewise, are also multifaceted. Some are focused on unpacking aspects of infrastructure bots sociality – examining the ways in which they facilitate, enable, and engage in social action. Others are tied to their role within systems of power, analyzing how bots might be used to perpetuate inequities or human rights violations. Finally, some theories of bot infrastructure explore their role in broader systems. They interrogate how bots contribute, implicitly and explicitly, to particular tasks and procedures on web-based platforms including social media sites.

Before bots hit the global news in 2016 due to political manipulation (Bessi & Ferrara, 2016; Hess, 2016), the general public either did not know about them or simply did not think about them. But as the internet and digital interactions (and the bots that make them possible) become more central to our lives, Hepp (2020) argues that scholars of media and communication ought to focus more research – theoretical and scientific – upon bots' role as "objects" of information transmission. He notes that when he advocates "the study of communicative robots," he means something "more than 'just' automated communication"; he argues that bots' work is "integrated into far-reaching and complex functionalities that [...] serve to collect data in the pursuit of recruiting communicative robots as agents in the projects of 'data colonialism' (Couldry & Mejias, 2019) and 'surveillance capitalism' (Zuboff, 2019)." In other words, bots are part of the infrastructure that countries and other powerful political actors use to present, represent, and encode the internet, conclusions drawn from the data therein, and particular cultural artifacts with power and specific meaning to people across the globe.[3] They are a means of controlling both the flow of information and understandings about information. Digital automation also plays a role in facilitating persistent online tracking of users' behaviors (surveillance) and selling of adverts and other products (capitalism).

As we've mentioned in previous chapters, bot web traffic makes up around 40 percent of all activity on the internet (Hughes, 2019), and only 20 percent of that bot traffic comes from "bad" or malicious bots (Osborne, 2019). Bots built for a wide variety of tasks are both ubiquitous on the web and integral to its functioning. As you've learned in previous chapters, bots carry out all sorts of social, commercial, and political work. As Punzalan (2017) points out, they also play a crucial role in digital archival work. Much of the time, bots are doing work that people don't want to do, because it is repetitive, boring, or not economically sensible. This unglamorous labor is often essential to the day-to-day running of websites and platforms across the internet. Because of this, many scholars have worked to show the importance of infrastructural bots, arguing that at bottom, they make it possible for humans to live more seamless online lives. Bots aren't just important to the technical success of digital systems, they are important to the social success of community systems.

Bots operating mostly behind-the-scenes are integral to the upkeep of extremely popular websites like Wikipedia and Reddit. The relationships of these bots to their builders, the sites on which they operate, and the other users with which they interact are complicated. Wikipedia, for example, must balance a back-end collaborative network of volunteer editors with a front-end encyclopedia with over 308 active language editions, and bots play an important role in coordinating this (Wikipedia, 2021). Geiger theorizes the role of Wikipedia bots in terms of bespoke code, which he defines as "code that runs alongside a platform or system, rather than being integrated into server-side codebases by individuals with privileged access to the server" (2014, p. 342). In other words, Wikipedia users can build bots that help to maintain the online encyclopedia without actually having to work for the platform. So, this is a parallel relationship rather than a hierarchical one; bespoke code (like that driving the off-server Wikipedia bots that are so crucial to the functioning of the site) upends the usual power dynamics between bots and their makers or hosts. For Geiger, the concept of bespoke code challenges the idea that the organization who owns a given server has complete control over code that facilitates communication (2014). His model suggests that to audit or understand a given platform's code – and the power underlying it or enabled by it – our inquiries must be "relational, networked, infrastructural" and "situated in many different kinds of spaces" beyond the server farm (2014, p. 352). For Geiger, the complex origins and ownership of the Wikipedia bots that mediate interaction on the site bring up critical questions about the "sociality of software" (2014, p. 353).

Long et al. (2017) take an HCI approach to exploring the role of bots on Reddit. Bots on Reddit serve a variety of functions, from moderating particular subreddits to replying to user comments. Long et al. therefore "set out to examine the qualities and functionalities of [Reddit] bots and the practical and social challenges surrounding their creation and use" (p. 3488). Their findings indicate that users on the platform – ranging from novices engaging in their first interactions with bots to the experts that build them – have very divergent expectations and understandings of their capabilities. On some subreddits, bots are programmed to carry out actions that the wider Reddit community sees as inappropriate; there is a seeming lack of standardization (both of bots and opinions about what bots should do) across the site as a whole. Long et al. argue that these misunderstandings and misuses of Reddit bots raise larger questions for communication-oriented bots online as they become more common. They underscore the need for "social responsibility in bot development" (p. 3497) and for continuing research into the contextual appropriateness of particular bot behaviors.

Bots also serve as infrastructure for democratically engaged political efforts. According to Woolley and Hwang (2015), bots can serve as civic prostheses or as social scaffolding; they can introduce previously unconnected social groups, encourage democratic engagement, shield protected or marginalized groups from harassment, and critique injustice. While bots can be used for manipulation, they can equally be used for good. As they note, bots are neither "good" nor "bad" simply by virtue of being bots: "the failure of a 'good' bot is a failure of design, not a failure of automation." In other words, when a bot designed to do "good" does "bad" things – such as Tay – that is because it wasn't given the right instructions, not simply because it was automated. Instead, they argue, "our discourse [on bots] would be more productive if it focused on the qualities that make bots the right tool for the job from a social and ethical standpoint, rather than ceding the promise of this technology to those who would use them for ill." Similarly, Woolley (2020b) points out that while scholarly focus has most recently been on the political misuse of bots, their potential for furthering democracy still remains, and this potential should be studied in more detail.

Conclusion

We still have a long way to go in our theorization of bots and their role in our culture. As the literature, ideas, and arguments in this chapter make clear, bots are important to the social and technical layers of the internet – and of life more generally – in complicated ways. But we still do not know where our current understanding of bot theory ends, and where we go from here. Perhaps the next hot topics will be the philosophy of "automated social actors," digital "proxies," or "symbiotic" computational systems. New methods would be welcome, particularly studies that set empirical analyses of bot actions and interactions alongside theorization of their unique social positioning on particular platform and across the wider web. Interrogation of the role of bots in the multi-platform, multi-lingual, spread of information and disinformation, for instance, could shed crucial light upon global influence operations and, relatedly, upon issues such as polarization, online "noise," conspiracy theory, trolling, and hate. We must build better understandings of the particular affordances of bots, in this regard, versus more intimate tactics such as the deployment of human influencers.

Scholars should continue to study how unexpected bot actions are tied to builders' biases and intentions, other users' machinations, and – most intriguingly – bots' own intelligence (or lack thereof). This latter point brings up one of the most popular issues around how we think about bots: their relationship with artificial intelligence, machine learning, and their often discussed "ethical" use and design. Scholars should continue to explore these topics, particularly the implications of AI bots for society. We need more work in pragmatically sorting out bots' capabilities with respect to AI and less work over-selling AI as the harbinger of some technoutopia – a misstep that would mimic earlier hype about the democratic potentials of social media (Morozov, 2010). We must also think beyond so-called "ethical" frameworks and toward systems of understanding bots and AI that are grounded in less subjectivity. For instance, how might we understand such systems in relationship to racial equity? Scholars, including Noble (2018), have paved the way for this work, but a great deal remains to be done. Such work ought also to look to the role of bots and AI as they relate to broader social equality and human rights.

As the use of automated human avatars (which stand in for real people) increases (Takahashi, 2020), so will the blurring of the line between people and bots. We need more research and theorization of human–bot "cyborgs" in order to understand the social and technical intricacies of hybrid digital-human actors and, as Woolley (2020b) points out, the ever more vague distinction between humans and machines will lead to all sorts of questions about reality, fact, and truth. Haraway (1991) provides a strong theoretical framework for understanding techno-human hybridization as a space where traditional boundaries and ideas about binary distinctions between nature and culture are challenged. For instance, she argues that cyborgs are "post-gender" and, as such, present promise for continued feminist theorization that blurs binary distinctions about identity. As she and others (Davisson & Booth, 2018; Gunkel, 2012; Floridi, 2014; Luke, 2018) suggest, we must continue to think through digital hybrid ethics, complicating rather than further rigidly defining it, in order to understand new "creatures" that emerge as technology and people further blend together. As Booch

(2016) argues, as we progress in developing machines built in the human image – and as we consider our fears about "super-intelligent AI" – we must endeavor to design and build AI tools engrained with the best features of humanity, rather than our worst ones.

7

Conclusion
The Future of Bots

In the past six decades, bots have helped to transform human communication and human–computer interaction. They've helped us navigate and make sense of a vast and ever-expanding internet, transformed how transactions are carried out in the commercial and financial sector, been deployed to boost activism, repression, and propaganda in the digital age, and evolved before our eyes in the latest wave of AI progress under deep learning. Simply put, our world is different because bots are in it. Bots are hugely widespread online, and they are integral to the functioning of our day-to-day lives in this modern hyperconnected world. Even the lives of people in places with little connectivity, whether by inequity or choice, are affected by the actions of bots upstream. Though they can be easy to miss, ambient in our everyday lives, they are crucial to many of the socio-technical systems that most people around the globe rely upon in some way, shape, or form (Aarts & Wichert, 2009).

Bots are an embodiment of the fact that computing is at its heart as much a social endeavor as a technical one. We can even see the social and human nature of computing and technology in the roots of many technological words: *digital* comes from the Latin for "finger" (digitus), which we use to count; *statistics* derive their name from being a study of the "state"; and in the early days of computing, English speakers referred to the computer as an "electric brain" (Mandarin Chinese still uses this term for computers; 電腦 diànnǎo). These linguistic traces reflect the long entwinement of social history with technological history. Our technologies are *always* embedded with social values in their design, whether or not technologists and developers know it when they create these tools.

There are still many questions about the specifics of how bots will evolve in the future, but we can make out some general contours. To conclude this book, we briefly address key future questions in bot policy, bot ethics, and bot research, the answers to which will indelibly shape our political, informational, social, commercial, and technological worlds.

The Future of Bot Development and Evolution

Several AI subfields hold great promise for transforming the capabilities and functionalities of bots in the future.

NLP

First, advances in NLP would be transformative for bots. NLP advances could spark rapid evolution of audio-based open-domain chatbots, which would allow what is called "pervasive conversational user interfaces" (CUIs) – voice-based interfaces, which are always listening for your instructions and can carry them out accurately. CUIs would radically transform how humans interact with computers. In many applications, talking to a computer could come to essentially replace using a mouse and keyboard as the main forms of human input.

Advances in NLP could also drive the development of medical chatbots. Chatbots are already being used in modest ways to supplement psychological treatment. Tools like Woebot, Wysa, and Youper are transparent chatbots that recommend cognitive behavioral therapy (CBT) techniques to address them (Zarka, 2018). Studies have shown that users enjoy chatting with these bots, and doing so has helped to reduce users' depressive symptoms (Fitzpatrick et al., 2017). The idea of using bots to improve patients' mental health was a dream of Kenneth Colby, a colleague of ELIZA creator Joseph Weizenbaum (Leonard, 1997, pp. 56–57). Colby hoped that bots could make psychotherapy more widely available in areas without access to high-quality mental health care (Hall, 2019). Lack of access to mental health services is a serious problem in most parts of the world today.

Synthetic media

Another area of bot and AI development to watch is *synthetic media*. These are videos, photographs, and text that are entirely computer-generated using AI, and sometimes referred to as "deepfakes." Deepfakes, created by automation using AI techniques, could have dire implications for the future of disinformation. Several concerning incidents have already occurred. Deepfake profile photos have been used to create fraudulent Twitter and Facebook accounts to be used in disinformation campaigns (Nimmo et al., 2019). In another case, a college student used GPT-3 to make a blog that was entirely computer-generated, and an article from the blog trended as the most popular news article on Y-Combinator's *Hacker News*, a news and discussion forum popular with Silicon Valley engineers and tech-savvy computer hobbyists (Hao, 2020; Porr, 2020). In theory, this is an audience that should be more skilled at spotting bot-generated content than the average internet user, but the quality of GPT-3's mimicry of blogposts fooled even them. Bots that could create millions of convincingly human fake news stories in minutes would represent a marked escalation of the current disinformation crisis that we have yet to fully solve.

Semantic Web

One of the most promising future applications of bots is Tim Berners-Lee's vision of the Semantic Web – an information environment that will "bring structure to the meaningful content of Web pages"; with bots "roaming from page to page ... carry[ing] out sophisticated tasks for users," which we briefly discussed in Chapters 4 and 5 (Berners-Lee et al., 2001). While computers, bots, and agents are already capable of visiting websites and retrieving documents on the World Wide Web, they are still unable to truly grasp the underlying meaning, or the semantics, behind those sites. This is because the World Wide Web is primarily organized and designed for human consumption; it was devised to make documents available to people. The Semantic Web would instead be designed for machines. It would be a machine-readable and machine-interpretable representation of the world that enables agents to understand and process information and to engage in "automated reasoning" about the world through knowledge representation (Berners-Lee et al., 2001; O'Brien, 2020). Berners-Lee envisions semi-autonomous programs, or *agents*, that are able to parse the meaning of information on the web and carry out independent tasks in order to simplify users' lives. On the Semantic Web, these agents, or bots, are envisioned as social creatures, capable of interacting with human users or other bots in order to help drive understanding of data and the world. On the Semantic Web, bots will be able to answer questions, schedule appointments, and process information efficiently so that humans don't have to.

While this vision is as of yet unrealized, the development of open standards for the Semantic Web, along with the emergence of conversational AI assistants, bots, and the Internet of Things, have brought us a step closer (Pomerantz, 2015, pp. 153–186).[1] Along with AI itself, the Semantic Web promises to transform the way humans understand the world and live in their daily lives. Indeed, according to Berners-Lee, this "web of data" has the potential to be even more revolutionary than the internet itself, moving us "from the Web of today to a Web in which machine reasoning will be ubiquitous and devastatingly powerful" (Berners-Lee, 1998).

Autonomous agents with advanced AI, traveling the Semantic Web and interacting with users via CUIs, could transform our world as surely as the invention of the internet itself has. Whether these ideas will be realized remains to be seen, but it is clear that AI and bots that use it will continue to have a transformative impact on our world, the world of bots, and the ways in which the two intersect. As bots and AI evolve in the coming decades, they will bring the host of social and ethical questions we explore below.

Future Questions for Bot Policy

Most of the world now accepts that online social bots are a problem in our information space and, in recent years, many have sought to address the problem. We are firm believers that targeted, well-crafted legislation against specific malicious uses of bots would be a step in the right direction. We also believe that overly broad legislation could be just as dangerous, and potentially oppressive, as no legislation at all. A blanket ban on bots in particular would transform the internet as we know it today; as this book has shown, bots are incredibly useful and diverse, and the internet simply would not exist without them.

Recent attempts at bot legislation in the state of California have illustrated some of the dangers of overly broad bot policy. The Bolstering Online Transparency (BOT) bill, SB 1001, was signed into law in July 2019. This policy requires bots active in the state of California to be transparent – to label themselves as bots – in most online spaces in which they interact with humans, particularly those in which they comment on political topics or attempt to influence voting behavior. While the intentions behind this bill were good, experts across the board agreed that this legislation was overly broad in its definitions and could stifle human users' speech in contexts where it was impossible to determine whether an account was automated (DiResta, 2019; Lamo &

Calo, 2018; Williams, 2018). We are strong supporters of bot transparency (all bots should label themselves as such) and of targeted legislation prohibiting the use of bots for political messaging, but overly broad laws such as these can do as much harm to our information environment as malicious bots themselves.

Perhaps the most central task for bot policy – and future election communications law more generally – is to legally define a bright line between fair digital campaigning and manipulative voter manipulation. We do not underestimate the difficulty of this task, but we know that it absolutely must be done. If the past decade has taught us anything, it is that anything is fair game in online electioneering when there are no laws or regulations prohibiting malicious uses of technology to manipulate voters. Unfortunately, what is good for election campaigners and social media companies often runs directly counter to what is good for voters – and for democracy. These "divergent incentives" are the root of the problem. Until a bright line is drawn to define legally what constitutes deceptive and manipulative behavior, citizens will get the raw end of the deal. These laws could be modeled on the legal definitions of other hazy concepts such as "fair dealing," "bad faith," and "usury" (Calo, 2014).

Future Ethical Questions

Recent evolutions in bots and AI have brought with them a tide of ethical questions for the future. One question that currently has no clear answer is: Who holds responsibility when a bot or machine results in physical harm to another? As we saw in Chapter 6, after Dutch programmer Jeffry van der Goot deployed the Twitter bot Jeffry_ebooks in 2015, the bot randomly made a death threat to another bot, and van der Goot was visited by police (Hill, 2015). More recently, self-driving cars have caused deaths (Wooldridge, 2020, pp. 151–152). Whose fault is this? Reasonable but consistent means of ensuring accountability in such cases must be determined; this is an important regulatory question for the future.

The same question extends to harms that are not physical. Another key area of concern is ensuring that AI systems guard against bias (Crawford, 2017). These issues become even more acute with "black box" algorithms such as deep learning systems, which operate opaquely – meaning that there is no way to explain the logic behind decisions they make. Regulatory measures, as well as sensible design that never puts black box algorithms at the center of key human decisions, are critical for guarding against such harms.

Accountability and data integrity lie at the core of the concerns explored above. Another key ethical concern is access itself. As bots and AI continue to transform and streamline aspects of daily life, access to these tools could increasingly determine standards of living. Of course, "access" means, in part, whether you can find or afford particular hardware or software. But it also extends to representation itself. For example, NLP research focuses primarily on languages with many speakers and large corpora of data to work with. According to two NLP researchers, "Most of today's NLP research focuses on 20 of the 7000 languages of the world, leaving the vast majority understudied" (Magueresse et al., 2020). Most of the world's 7,000 languages lack even basic NLP support (Monaco & Woolley, 2019). While linguistic support for the world's most spoken languages has made great strides in the past few years, NLP support for most languages on earth is in its infancy, if it exists at all. In order for computers to begin to parse, manipulate, and produce human language, a vast amount of human legwork needs to be done in the form of formal linguistic study. With the majority of the world's 7,000 languages lacking even a standardized writing system, most languages do not have adequate AI support, and will not for quite some time (Monaco & Woolley, 2019). In a future of widespread CUIs, AI assistants, and a functioning Semantic Web, most people will need to learn a foreign language to interface with the robots that can transform our lives. In this environment, the question of which languages are supported becomes one with strong political, social, and even economic implications. It will be crucial to promote investment, linguistic research, and technological development in multiple low-resource languages around the world, to ensure that they are supported and distribute the benefits of technological advancement more evenly.

On the flipside, widespread CUIs, AI assistants, and more efficient parsing of human language data through NLP breakthroughs, particularly advances in ASR and computational semantics – advances that would drive computers to actually parse the meaning of spoken sentences – would undoubtedly have grave implications for mass surveillance. As it stands right now, computers are much better at parsing written text data than speech data. In either case, however, they are not skilled at understanding the general *meaning* of sentences or language data without domain-specific knowledge embedded in them through schemas like the ontologies and knowledge graphs we discussed in Chapter 5. Were computers to gain the ability to *understand* the meaning of phrases autonomously, mass digital surveillance could become much more oppressive. For example, it could be easier for governments to locate dissidents who said something negative about them, and persecute them. Companies could also use the same tools to try to identify potential corporate whistleblowers or defectors. The grave implications of these technologies must be planned for and designed to minimize these potential harms.

Another issue central to the future of bots is guarding against unethical uses of AI-powered bots in the information space. As we discussed in our chapter on political bots and computational propaganda, most of the political bots in the past decade have been dumb bots that used simplistic programming – things like ELIZA-based chatbot functionality and simple heuristics to create and promote their content.

Even these rudimentary strategies were able to successfully manipulate the political conversation through algorithmic gaming, in particular by making content trend with frequent interactions. In our chapter on bots and AI, we saw that this era may be coming to an end. The college student who created an entirely AI-generated blog that trended at the top of Hacker News was a clear signal of the dangers presented by the spread of AI capable of advanced language generation. Bots that can convincingly generate millions of stories per minute on any input topic would create disinformation on a scale unlike anything we can imagine today. Combined with AI-enhanced analysis of online data for individual microtargeting, the possibilities are, quite frankly, terrifying (Neudert, 2018).

In addition to the NLP advances we've seen with GPT-3, the development of deepfake and synthetic media brings new questions about our perceptions of reality and ability to separate truth from fiction. Questions about how to best develop and distribute these systems abound. On one hand, keeping them in the hands of a limited number of trusted entities guards against widespread abuse; on the other hand, this hands over even more power to the technological sector, which already holds more power than any other organization in human history.

These concerns do not only exist at the nation state level but at the individual level. With the recent growth of peer-to-peer disinformation and harassment campaigns that leverage bots and AI technologies, abuse of AI on an interpersonal level is also likely to proliferate. Red flags have begun to appear in recent years. We are seeing new companies offering customers the ability to target loved ones with persuasive messages, offering to nudge clients' loved ones into losing weight or converting religions using shady digital tactics (Poulsen, 2019; Stoppard, 2018). One especially troubling abuse is a Telegram deepfake bot that generates synthetic naked images of women (Burgess, 2020). This bot has been used to generate fake nude images of real women from malicious users around the globe, seeking revenge or leverage for exploitation. While these images aren't real, the consequences are: they can cause serious harm to the subjects of the photos, even if they are proven to be fake. It is crucial that we design regulations and technologies to prevent abuse of AI functionality to ensure that we reap more good than harm from this technology.

The Future Study of Bots

We still have a lot of work to do to understand how bots interact with technical systems, humans, and the world. Researchers who want to build that understanding should focus on several areas: bots and AI, the ethical use of bots, bot agency, bots and communication, bots and politics, bots and commerce, and the use of bots as social scaffolding or tools beneficial to society. Each of these issues brings with it several questions.

Scholars examining bots and AI must work to explain and demystify the relationship between the two. Over the last several years, journalists, researchers, and other purveyors of information and understanding have framed bots as smart AI tools. This might not seem like a big deal but, in fact, it can lead to fear and misconception. It can also make it harder to generate the right solutions to problems caused by the misuse of bots. Many bots used in politics, for instance, are not coded with AI or machine learning at all; they aren't built to engage in realistic conversations or learn from their surroundings, but simply to like or share content, follow people, or repeat the same phrases or hashtags over and over. They are blunt instruments, but they get the job done for the propagandists and manipulators who use them. Wrongly suggesting that such bots use AI adds an unnecessary layer of complexity and apprehension to the mix, particularly as the public works to understand the social use of bots. It makes bots into boogeymen, like the Terminator or HAL 9000, rather than allowing people to understand what these political bots are: a simple misuse of fairly rudimentary software. Researchers and journalists must accurately contextualize how AI is used by bots, particularly when bots are used maliciously.

Of course, some ethical issues around bots are raised by AI in digital automation, and researchers must carefully consider the implications of the tools they are building. For example, when building AI chatbots, we must consider how they might be misused – leveraged by criminals, hate-groups, or despots. We must also think through as many consequences as possible. For example, if you are training a machine learning chatbot to, say, spot trolling, you must consider who is tagging alleged harassment, and whether you have ensured that reporting cannot be misused for further harassment. You must also ensure that the programmers, as a group, represent diverse communities. A bot intended to help solve a serious issue can quickly become part of the problem if it's designed and trained by only white men between the ages of 22 and 40. Other ethical questions include how to monitor and regulate bots used in high-frequency trading. We cannot allow financial or technical processes, automated or not, to be unmonitored and unregulated, and their processes and decisions must be transparent. Bots' workings and intentions are often (sometimes purposefully) obscured by their complexity. But researchers, journalists, civil society groups, and others must work to translate the problems associated with bots so that everyone affected by them – which by now you know is basically everyone – can understand what they are doing and why they are doing it. Without this kind of transparency, it will be impossible to implement the regulation, policy, and processes needed to curb unethical bot use.

STS and HCI scholars have made great headway in understanding the relationships between society and technology, and the problems they can cause (Dourish, 2004; Suchman, 2006; Winner, 1980). They've also theorized that some technological artifacts – including bots – have a kind of agency (Latour, 2007; Law & Hassard, 1999; Kono, 2013). But this research is still in its infancy; there are still many, many questions around how bots are situated in the social world and how much agency they have. To use bots to benefit rather than harm society, we must consider these questions. Ethical chatbots will also be more effective, better designed, and more useful chatbots. A clear understanding about what bots (and AI) are and are not will allow journalists and thought leaders – who play such a pivotal role in disseminating knowledge to the public – to give clear, accurate accounts of technological developments in automated technologies. And continuing research into bot agency will also help us understand how agency may apply to other software and hardware tools – particularly AI, which must be understood as it develops and is implemented for a wide variety of purposes across the globe.

As a society, we must not accept malicious uses of bots, for any reason – political, financial, informational, or otherwise. Researchers must continue to study and expose manipulative, underhanded, and inequitable uses of bots, and suggest solutions to the problems they identify; the same energy researchers put into drawing attention to, say, political misuse of bots must be put into combating such misuse, and generating socially beneficial uses of bots. But we must not fall into the trap of fighting fire with fire – of using armies of allegedly "democratic" bots to fight against armies of "authoritarian" bots, particularly if the so-called democratic bots are not transparent about their status as bots and about who made them.

Researchers have spent years using weapon and war-oriented metaphors (like the one we just used) to describe the political use of bots on social media and the digital spread of disinformation. But the idea that we are in a war on bots limits our ability to see bots' positive potential. There is tremendous room for bots to do good in society; the tools that can generate societal problems can also generate social solutions. We must begin to imagine ways in which bots can serve as social scaffolding or civic remedies. Bots are, after all, a reflection of the people who build and use them; we must work to instill our best qualities into them and to keep our worst qualities out.

Notes

CHAPTER 1 WHAT IS A BOT?

1 *Chatbot* has now become the most common term for conversational agents, but "chatterbot," a term coined by famous bot builder Michael Mauldin in the 1990s, was then a common term for the same phenomenon (Deryugina, 2010; Leonard, 1997, p. 4).
2 ELIZA's pattern matching and substitution methods work in the same way that "regular expressions" or "RegEx" work today. RegEx is a formal language for pattern-matching in human language. It is often used to help computers search for and detect pre-defined patterns in human language (words, sentences, phone numbers, URLs, etc.) as a pre-processing step for modern natural language processing programs (Jurafsky & Martin, 2018, pp. 9–10).
3 The fundamental importance of bots as a sense-making and infrastructural part of the internet is one of the primary reasons why laws or regulations advocating a blanket ban on bots would destroy the modern web as we know it.
4 Of course, modern computer networks and the internet use dozens of protocols in addition to HTTP, such as the transmission control protocol (TCP), internet protocol (IP), and simple mail transfer protocol (SMTP) – all used millions of times every day. All of these small parts are necessary cogs that make up the machinery of the modern internet (Frystyk, 1994; Shuler, 2002).
5 The first graphical MUDs did not begin to appear until the mid 1980s (Castronova, 2005, p. 55).
6 Early web indexing bots were also called by other names, including "wanderers," "worms," "fish," "walkers," "knowbots," and "web robots," among others (Gudivada et al., 1997).
7 While HTML is the primary language that web developers use to build webpages, other languages, such as CSS and JavaScript,

provide very important secondary functions for websites and are essential building blocks for modern websites.

8   Today, the ubiquity of web-indexing crawler bots on the World Wide Web are one aspect of what distinguishes the everyday internet from what is known as the *"dark web."* In contrast, the dark web is an alternative form of the internet, which requires additional software, protocols, and technical knowledge to access – Tor, I2P, Freenet, ZeroNet, GNUnet, are but a few of the possible tools that can be used to access the dark web (Gehl, 2018). While security enthusiasts, researchers, and cybersecurity firms can build crawler bots to explore the dark web, large-scale centralized search engines like Google do not exist on the dark web. Navigation of the dark web is therefore mainly conducted through word-of-mouth within small communities, or on smaller scale search engines that resemble the "web directories" of the early internet. Much of the dark web is made of sites that are not indexed by crawler bots at all. Much of the activity that takes place on the dark web is meant to be clandestine (such as online crime, illegal marketplaces, and censorship circumvention websites and tools). The dark web also allows users and publishers to remain anonymous online.

9   Martijn Koster, one of the most prominent bot developers and bot thinkers in the 1990s, also built a database of known crawlers (or "Web Robots," in the parlance of the times) that is still online (Koster, n.d.).

10 The "deep web" is also a concept worth noting. Deep web sites are sites that require special permissions (such as a password) to access and cannot be read or seen without that access. For example, while facebook.com itself is indexable and readable from all search engines, particular Facebook users' profiles and posts may not be visible in search engine results due to individual privacy settings. So, while facebook.com itself is part of the clear web, unviewable and unindexed profiles would qualify as being part of the *deep web*.

11 The Robot Exclusion Standard is also known as the Robot Exclusion Protocol.

12 In addition to APIs and headless browser automation tools, there is a third option for programming online bots: Graphical User Interface (GUI) automation packages like Python's *pyautogui* library. These packages enable users to program automated behavior on a local computer, automating things like cursor movement and keyboards (Kiehl, 2012; Sweigart, 2015, pp.

438–439). However, like using automated browser software, this is a more time-consuming and difficult way to build a bot that generally requires developers with significant technical skill.
13 As Gorwa and Guilbeault note, researchers sometimes choose to write social bot as one word, *socialbot* (2018).
14 The term *propaganda* itself is similar in this way – while the English term carries an exclusively negative connotation, in other languages such as Chinese, the term for "propaganda" (宣傳) is more neutral in tone, with a sense of general promotion or public relations of any sort (Jack, 2017).

CHAPTER 2 BOTS AND SOCIAL LIFE

1 XiaoIce was a Chinese-language precursor to @Tay, Microsoft's English-language Twitter bot experiment. Tay emulated a human female and talked about all sorts of things with social media users in China. While @Tay went wrong [with a Western-centric focus/ a flawed corpus/ a set of culturally offensive responses/ a "personality" almost as annoying as Clippy], she reveals the broad social capacity of bots. The code for @Tay has been used to build bots that generate original poetry and songs, read audio books, design cityscapes, host radio and TV programs, write news articles, and share updates on financial markets.
2 The internet was originally created by the US military, which worked with academic institutions to create a network of connected machines; the best-known antecedent to today's web was the ARPANET (Advanced Research Projects Agency Network). Turner (2006) provides an excellent description of the early days of the net, and the unique, divergent cultures (military, academic, and 1960s anti-establishment) from which it sprang.
3 Many computer and cognitive scientists have argued that the Turing Test measures only a narrow definition of intelligence, and that even digital entities that passed the test might not be truly sentient or intelligent (Marie del Prado, 2015).
4 "Chatbot" and "social bot" are not interchangeable terms. Some bots that are not built to directly interact conversationally with people or other bots can be considered social bots, because they can create social outcomes and can take part in human–machine "symbiosis" (Neff & Nagy, 2016b).
5 Bots are, however, very useful for some aspects of investigative journalism, such as combing through and sorting large amounts

of data – huge tranches of released government emails or the complex financial information of companies or individuals under investigation. For example, Quartz has built programs that can search massive databases of financial leaks and corporate information in order to find corruption and fraud (Merrill, 2020).

6 Francois Triquet (2016) of SAP Conversational AI offers a more nuanced parsing of game bots versus NPCs (non-player characters): "a 'bot,' short for robot, is a computer program controlling a virtual character and imitating human behavior. The NPC is a game character controlled by a computer." For Triquet, the bot mimics a character that would otherwise be played by a human user.

7 O'Reilly (Bruner, 2016), a popular media firm based in the Bay Area, claimed that 2016 was "shaping up to be the year of the Bot." It points to the fact that Microsoft Satya Nadella said, that year, that "bots [were] going to be the new apps."

Chapter 3 Bots and Political Life

1 There is a subtle but important difference between acquiring data through an API and acquiring it through scraping. APIs can be thought of as a sanctioned means of gathering *selected* data from a website – through the API, the website (or platform) owner controls what information you can access, as well as how much of it, by pre-defining limitations. Scraping data is a means of collecting *any* visible information from a website using a bot you have programmed to copy and save the information, whether or not the website owner permits you to do so. For example, Twitter has a free API that will allow users to gather certain data, but not just any data – the API is subject to oversight and limitations imposed by the company (rate limits). You can use the Twitter API to gather a user's most recent 3,200 tweets, for example, but you cannot gather more than those tweets. This limitation is a deliberate choice by the platform, presumably meant to protect users' privacy. The API also allows you to gather information about certain tweets, such as how many likes or retweets the tweet has. It will not, however, allow you to collect a list of *which users* liked the tweet. Again, these are deliberate choices Twitter has made. If you are able to view the information that you'd like to collect in a browser

(such as likes on a tweet, or tweets that were made before a user's most recent 3,200 tweets), you could program a bot to scrape that information from the browser. This type of scraping is a violation of Twitter's terms of service (and quite possibly the law), but it is technically relatively trivial for bots and bot designers (Monaco & Arnaudo, 2020), and it is difficult and expensive for companies to detect and prevent.

2 Non-digital, non-online automation is also used for activism – and for fraud. Spammers, scammers, and activists alike often automate phone calls to target specific areas, a practice known as *robocalling*. In the 2018 US mid-terms, one right-wing extremist used spoofed local numbers to automate thousands of robocalls targeting voters with racist messages and exploiting local news events to sow divisions in communities. In 2020, the US FCC fined the man behind these calls nearly $13 million USD for violating the law (Federal Communications Commission, 2020; Wilson, 2020).

CHAPTER 4 BOTS AND COMMERCE

1 [*Sic*].
2 After Tay, the company released a similar AI bot, Zo (@zochats). While she was presented as something of a successor to Tay (Microsoft, 2016b), Zo was in fact more closely modeled on XiaoIce, the far-reaching multi-platform Asian language chatbot discussed in Chapter 2. XiaoIce had engaged with over 40 million people for several years and had never behaved like Tay (Lee).
3 *Business Insider* makes a distinction between customer service bots and virtual assistant chatbots (VACs). Both provide "information, services, and assistance about web pages, and support a wide range of applications in business, educations, government, healthcare, and entertainment." But VACs are more generally used for helping businesses internally rather than helping clients or customers directly. VACs' utility for companies is clear: "VACs can carry out a range of tasks to better organize an office such as creating lists, scheduling any appointments or reminders, opening software, or activating smart devices."
4 I.e. when they discover pricing deviation between two currencies in which a trade of one for another would make the user money.

Chapter 6 Theorizing the Bot

1 And, on social media platforms (for instance), the algorithms that dictate which people see or interact with the bot.
2 These good or bad actions are, of course, morally and culturally contextual.
3 Therefore (hypothetically) allowing countries such as the US or China to control presentation of online information to people in Malaysia or Zambia.

Chapter 7 Conclusion: The Future of Bots

1 eXtensible markup language (XML), the Resource Description Framework (RDF), Facebook's Open Graph Protocol, Google's Knowledge Graph, and schema.org are but a few examples of open standards (Pomerantz, 2015, pp. 153–186).

References

Aamoth, D. (2014, June 9). Interview with Eugene Goostman, the Fake Kid Who Passed the Turing Test. *Time*. https://time.com/2847900/eugene-goostman-turing-test/

Aarts, E. and Wichert, R. (2009) Ambient Intelligence. In Bullinger, H. J. (ed.) *Technology Guide*. Springer, Berlin, Heidelberg. https://doi.org/10.1007/978-3-540-88546-7_47

Abokhodair, N., Yoo, D., & McDonald, D. W. (2015). Dissecting a Social Botnet: Growth, Content and Influence in Twitter. *Proceedings of the 18th ACM Conference on Computer Supported Cooperative Work & Social Computing*, 839–851. https://doi.org/10.1145/2675133.2675208

Abu Rajab, M., Zarfoss, J., Monrose, F., & Terzis, A. (2006). A Multifaceted Approach to Understanding the Botnet Phenomenon. *Proceedings of the 6th ACM SIGCOMM Conference on Internet Measurement*, 41–52. https://doi.org/10.1145/1177080.1177086

Adiwardana, D., Luong, M.-T., So, D. R., Hall, J., Fiedel, N., Thoppilan, R., Yang, Z., Kulshreshtha, A., Nemade, G., Lu, Y., & Le, Q. V. (2020). Towards a Human-like Open-Domain Chatbot. *ArXiv:2001.09977 [Cs, Stat]*. http://arxiv.org/abs/2001.09977

Adiwardana, D. & Luong, T. (2020, January 28). Towards a Conversational Agent that Can Chat About ... Anything. *Google AI Blog*. http://ai.googleblog.com/2020/01/towards-conversational-agent-that-can.html

Agencies (2013, October 24). Samsung Fined in Taiwan for "Dirty Tricks" Campaign Against Smartphone Rival HTC. *Guardian*. https://www.theguardian.com/technology/2013/oct/24/samsung-fined-taiwan-campaign-against-smartphone-htc

Aiello, L. M., Deplano, M., Schifanella, R., & Ruffo, G. (2014). People are Strange When You're a Stranger: Impact and Influence of Bots on Social Networks. *ArXiv:1407.8134 [Physics]*. http://arxiv.org/abs/1407.8134

Akrich, M. (1987). Comment décrire les objets techniques? *Techniques et culture*, 9, 49. https://halshs.archives-ouvertes.fr/halshs-00005830

Albayrak, A. & Parkinson, J. (2013, September 16). Turkey's

References

Government Forms 6,000-Member Social Media Team. *Wall Street Journal*. https://online.wsj.com/article/SB10001424127887323527004579079151479634742.html

Alexander, L. (2015, April 2). Social Network Analysis Reveals Full Scale of Kremlin's Twitter Bot Campaign. *Global Voices*. https://globalvoices.org/2015/04/02/analyzing-kremlin-twitter-bots/

Alpaydin, E. (2016). *Machine Learning: The New AI*. MIT Press.

Ananny, Mi. & Finn, M. (2015). Public News Bots? Creating Networked News Time in Automated Journalism. Annual Meeting for the Society for the Social Studies of Science., Denver, CO.

Assenmacher, D., Clever, L., Frischlich, L., Quandt, T., Trautmann, H., & Grimme, C. (2020). Demystifying Social Bots: On the Intelligence of Automated Social Media Actors. *Social Media + Society*, 6(3), 2056305120939264. https://doi.org/10.1177/2056305120939264

Associated Press (2019). AP to Grow Major League Soccer Coverage with Automated Stories. *Associated Press*. https://www.ap.org/press-releases/2019/ap-to-grow-major-league-soccer-coverage-with-automated-stories

Backspace (2015). NYPD edits (@NYPDedits) / Twitter. *Twitter*. https://twitter.com/NYPDedits

Baker, V. (2015). Battle of the Bots. *Index on Censorship*, 44(2), 127–129. https://doi.org/10.1177/0306422015591470

BBC News (2014, June 9). Computer AI Passes Turing Test in "World First." https://www.bbc.com/news/technology-27762088

Benner, K., Mazzetti, M., Hubbard, B., & Isaac, M. (2018, October 20). Saudis' Image Makers: A Troll Army and a Twitter Insider. *New York Times*. https://www.nytimes.com/2018/10/20/us/politics/saudi-image-campaign-twitter.html

Bergstrom, C. T. & West, J. D. (2020). *Calling Bullshit: The Art of Skepticism in a Data-Driven World*. Random House.

Berners-Lee, T. (1998, September). Semantic Web Road Map. *World Wide Web Consortium*. https://www.w3.org/DesignIssues/Semantic.html

Berners-Lee, T., Hendler, J., & Lassila, O. (2001, May). The Semantic Web. *Scientific American*. https://doi.org/10.1038/scientificamerican0501-34

Bessi, A. & Ferrara, E. (2016). Social Bots Distort the 2016 US Presidential Election Online Discussion. *First Monday*, 21(11). https://doi.org/10.5210/fm.v21i11.7090

Bobrow, D., Kaplan, R., Kay, M., Norman, D., Thompson, H. S., & Winograd, T. (1977). GUS, A Frame-Driven Dialog System. *Artif. Intell.* https://doi.org/10.1016/0004-3702(77)90018-2

Booch, G. (2016). *Don't Fear Superintelligent AI*. https://www.ted.com/talks/grady_booch_don_t_fear_superintelligent_ai

Borch, C. (2016). High-Frequency Trading, Algorithmic Finance and the Flash Crash: Reflections on Eventalization. *Economy and Society*, 45(3–4), 350–378. https://doi.org/10.1080/03085147.2016.1263034

Boshmaf, Y., Muslukhov, I., Beznosov, K., & Ripeanu, M. (2011). The Socialbot Network: When Bots Socialize for Fame and Money. 93–102. https://doi.org/10.1145/2076732.2076746

Bosker, B. (2014, June 9). Don't Believe the So-Called Turing Test Breakthrough | *HuffPost*. https://www.huffpost.com/entry/turing-test-eugene-goostman_n_5474457

botnerds (2020). Types of Bots: An Overview of Chatbot Diversity. botnerds.com. *Botnerds*. http://botnerds.com/types-of-bots/

BotSentinel.com (2020). *Bot Sentinel – About*. https://botsentinel.com/info/about

Bradshaw, S. & Howard, P. N. (2019). The Global Disinformation Order 2019 Global Inventory of Organised Social Media Manipulation (Working Paper 2019.2). Oxford Internet Institute. https://comprop.oii.ox.ac.uk/wp-content/uploads/sites/93/2019/09/CyberTroop-Report19.pdf

Brogan, P. (1993). *The Torturers' Lobby: How Human Rights-Abusing Nations Are Represented in Washington*. The Center for Public Integrity.

Brown, A. (2020, February 10). High-Frequency Trading Is Changing for the Better. *Bloomberg*. https://www.bloomberg.com/opinion/articles/2020-02-10/high-frequency-trading-is-changing-for-the-better

Brown, T. B., Mann, B., Ryder, N., Subbiah, M., Kaplan, J., Dhariwal, P., Neelakantan, A., Shyam, P., Sastry, G., Askell, A., Agarwal, S., Herbert-Voss, A., Krueger, G., Henighan, T., Child, R., Ramesh, A., Ziegler, D. M., Wu, J., Winter, C., ... Amodei, D. (2020). Language Models are Few-Shot Learners. *ArXiv:2005.14165 [Cs]*. http://arxiv.org/abs/2005.14165

Bruner, J. (2016, June 15). Why 2016 is Shaping Up to Be the Year of the Bot. *O'Reilly Media*. https://www.oreilly.com/radar/why-2016-is-shaping-up-to-be-the-year-of-the-bot/

Bucher, T. (2014). About a Bot: Hoax, Fake, Performance Art. *M/C Journal*, 17(3), Article 3. https://doi.org/10.5204/mcj.814

Bulut, E. & Yörük, E. (2017). Mediatized Populisms| Digital Populism: Trolls and Political Polarization of Twitter in Turkey. *International Journal of Communication*, 11(0), 25.

Bump, P. (2017, June 12). Analysis: Welcome to the Era of the

'Bot' as Political Boogeyman. *Washington Post.* https://www.washingtonpost.com/news/politics/wp/2017/06/12/welcome-to-the-era-of-the-bot-as-political-boogeyman/

Burgess, M. (2020, October 21). A Deepfake Porn Bot Is Being Used to Abuse Thousands of Women. *Wired.* https://www.wired.co.uk/article/telegram-deepfakes-deepnude-ai

Burling, S. (2012, June 15). CAPTCHA: The Story Behind Those Squiggly Computer Letters. https://phys.org/news/2012-06-captcha-story-squiggly-letters.html

Butler, W. (2019, January 17). What Happened to CongressEdits? The Thrilling Life and Untold Death of Twitter's Most Important Wikipedia Bot. *Wikipedian.* http://thewikipedian.net/2019/01/17/congressedits-twitter-suspended/

Callon, Michel (1986). *Mapping the Dynamics of Science and Technology: Sociology of Science in the Real World.* Macmillan Press.

Calo, R. (2014). Digital Market Manipulation. *George Washington Law Review,* 82, 995.

Castronova, E. (2005). *Synthetic Worlds The Business and Culture of Online Games.* University of Chicago Press.

Castronova, E. (2007). *Effects of Botting on World of Warcraft.* Indiana University. http://virtuallyblind.com/files/mdy/blizzard_msj_exhibit_7.pdf

Ceruzzi, P. E. (2012). *Computing: A Concise History.* MIT Press

Chen, A. (2015, June 2). The Agency. *New York Times.* https://www.nytimes.com/2015/06/07/magazine/the-agency.html

Chi, C. (2021, February 22). 12 of the Best AI Chatbots for 2021. *Hubspot Blog.* https://blog.hubspot.com/marketing/best-ai-chatbot

Cisco Talos Intelligence (2020, October). Email and Spam Data. https://talosintelligence.com/reputation_center/email_rep

Clayton, M. (2014, June 17). Ukraine Election Narrowly Avoided "Wanton Destruction" from Hackers. *Christian Science Monitor.* https://www.csmonitor.com/World/Passcode/2014/0617/Ukraine-election-narrowly-avoided-wanton-destruction-from-hackers

Colby, K. M., Hilf, F. D., Weber, S., & Kraemer, H. C. (1972). Turing-Like Indistinguishability Tests for the Validation of a Computer Simulation of Paranoid Processes. *Artificial Intelligence,* 3, 119–221.

Confessore, N., Dance, G. J. X., Harris, R., & Hansen, M. (2018, January 27). The Follower Factory. *New York Times.*

Cook, J. (2011a, August 1). Most of Newt Gingrich's Twitter Followers Are Fake. *Gawker.* http://gawker.com/5826645/most-of-newt-gingrichs-twitter-followers-are-fake

Cook, J. (2011b, August 2). Update: Only 92% of Newt Gingrich's Twitter Followers Are Fake. *Gawker.* http://gawker.com/5826960/update-only-92-of-newt-gingrichs-twitter-followers-are-fake

Couldry, N. & Mejias, U. A. (2019). Data Colonialism: Rethinking Big Data's Relation to the Contemporary Subject. *Television & New Media,* 20(4), 336–349. https://doi.org/10.1177/1527476418796632

Cox, J. (2014, July 10). These Bots Tweet When Government Officials Edit Wikipedia. *Vice Motherboard.* https://www.vice.com/en/article/pgaka8/these-bots-tweet-when-government-officials-edit-wikipedia

Crawford, K. (2017, October 17). Artificial Intelligence – With Very Real Biases. *Wall Street Journal.* https://www.wsj.com/articles/artificial-intelligencewith-very-real-biases-1508252717

Cresci, S. (2020, October). A Decade of Social Bot Detection. *Communications of the ACM.* https://cacm.acm.org/magazines/2020/10/247598-a-decade-of-social-bot-detection/fulltext

Cresci, S., Di Pietro, R., Petrocchi, M., Spognardi, A., & Tesconi, M. (2017). The Paradigm-Shift of Social Spambots: Evidence, Theories, and Tools for the Arms Race. *Proceedings of the 26th International Conference on World Wide Web Companion – WWW '17 Companion,* 963–972. https://doi.org/10.1145/3041021.3055135

DataDome (2020, January 13). How to Protect your Gaming or Gambling Website from Bad Bots. *DataDome.* https://datadome.co/bot-management-protection/how-to-protect-your-gaming-gambling-and-entertainment-sites-from-malicious-bots/

Davisson, A. & Booth, P. (2018). *Controversies in Digital Ethics.* Bloomsbury Publishing USA.

Deryugina, O. V. (2010). Chatterbots. *Scientific and Technical Information Processing,* 37(2), 143–147. https://doi.org/10.3103/S0147688210020097

Dewey, C. (2014, May 23). What Happens when @everyword Ends? *Washington Post.* https://www.washingtonpost.com/news/the-intersect/wp/2014/05/23/what-happens-when-everyword-ends/

Dhapola, S. (2021, January 25). How a Chatbot Helped Joe Biden Become US President. *The Indian Express.* https://indianexpress.com/article/technology/tech-news-technology/amplify-ai-chatbot-how-it-helped-joe-biden-become-us-president-7157578/

DiResta, R. (2019, July 24). A New Law Makes Bots Identify Themselves – That's the Problem. *Wired.* https://www.wired.com/story/law-makes-bots-identify-themselves/

DiResta, R., Little, J., Morgan, J., Neudert, L.-M., & Nimmo, B. (2017, November 2). The Bots That Are Changing Politics.

https://www.vice.com/en/article/mb37k4/twitter-facebook-google-bots-misinformation-changing-politics

Disawar, V. & Chang, J. (2021, December 31). Digital Organizing Tech: 2020 Investments and Learnings. *Medium.* https://vdisawar.medium.com

DoNotPay (2021). Save Time and Money with DoNotPay! *DoNotPay.* https://join.donotpay.com

Dourish, P. (2004). *Where the Action Is: The Foundations of Embodied Interaction* (new edn.). MIT Press.

Dubbin, R. (2013, November 14). The Rise of Twitter Bots. *The New Yorker.* https://www.newyorker.com/tech/annals-of-technology/the-rise-of-twitter-bots

Dzieza, J. (2019, February 1). Why CAPTCHAs Have Gotten so Difficult. *The Verge.* https://www.theverge.com/2019/2/1/18205610/google-captcha-ai-robot-human-difficult-artificial-intelligence

Economist (2016, March 2). After Moore's Law. *Technology Quarterly.* https://www.economist.com/technology-quarterly/2016-03-12/after-moores-law

Economist (2020, August 6). Artificial Intelligence – A New AI Language Model Generates Poetry and Prose. *Science & Technology.* https://www.economist.com/science-and-technology/2020/08/06/a-new-ai-language-model-generates-poetry-and-prose

Edwards, C., Edwards, A., Spence, P. R., & Shelton, A. K. (2014). Is that a Bot Running the Social Media Feed? Testing the Differences in Perceptions of Communication Quality for a Human Agent and a Bot Agent on Twitter. *Computers in Human Behavior, 33,* 372–376. https://doi.org/10.1016/j.chb.2013.08.013

Elish, M. C. & Hwang, T. (2016, September 29). An AI Pattern Language. *Data & Society.* https://www.datasociety.net/pubs/ia/AI_Pattern_Language.pdf

Elmer-Dewitt, P. (1993, December 6). Internet Article TIME International. *Time.* http://kirste.userpage.fu-berlin.de/outerspace/internet-article.html

Existor (2014, February 5). Deep Context Through Parallel Processing – *Existor.* https://www.existor.com/2014/02/05/deep-context-through-parallel-processing/

Federal Communications Commission (2020). FCC Proposes Nearly $13 Million Fine for Illegal Spoofed Robocalls. *FCC News.* https://docs.fcc.gov/public/attachments/DOC-362195A1.pdf

Fernandez, M. (2017, October 12). What it Means to Be an "Experimental Computer Poet." https://www.vice.com/en/article/8x8ppp/poetry-twitter-bots-best-twitter-bots-art-allison-parrish-everyword

Ferrara, E., Varol, O., Davis, C., Menczer, F., & Flammini, A. (2014). The Rise of Social Bots. https://doi.org/10.1145/2818717

Filipov, D. (2017, October 8). The Notorious Kremlin-Linked "Troll Farm" and the Russians Trying to Take it Down. *Washington Post*. https://www.washingtonpost.com/world/asia_pacific/the-notorious-kremlin-linked-troll-farm-and-the-russians-trying-to-take-it-down/2017/10/06/c8c4b160-a919-11e7-9a98-07140d2eed02_story.html

Fitzpatrick, K. K., Darcy, A., & Vierhile, M. (2017). Delivering Cognitive Behavior Therapy to Young Adults With Symptoms of Depression and Anxiety Using a Fully Automated Conversational Agent (Woebot): A Randomized Controlled Trial. *JMIR Mental Health*, 4(2), e7785. https://doi.org/10.2196/mental.7785

Flatow, I. (2011, April 22). Science Diction: The Origin Of The Word "Robot." In *Talk of the Nation*. NPR. https://www.npr.org/2011/04/22/135634400/science-diction-the-origin-of-the-word-robot

Floridi, L. (2014). Artificial Agents and their Moral Nature. In *The Moral Status of Technical Artifacts* (pp. 185–213). https://doi.org/10.1007/978-94-007-7914-3_11

Floridi, L. (2016, January 25). Humans Have Nothing to Fear from Intelligent Machines. *Financial Times*. https://www.ft.com/content/9a6b6536-c372-11e5-808f-8231cd71622e

Foner, L. N. (1993). What's An Agent, Anyway? A Sociological Case Study. http://www.upv.es/sma/teoria/agentes/what%20is%20an%20agent-foner.pdf

Foote, A. (2018, July 23). The Secret Internet War Over Bots. *Wired*. https://www.wired.com/story/scraper-bots-and-the-secret-internet-arms-race/

Ford, H., Dubois, E., & Puschmann, C. (2016). Keeping Ottawa Honest – One Tweet at a Time? Politicians, Journalists, Wikipedians and Their Twitter Bots. *International Journal of Communication*, 10(0), 24.

Forelle, M., Howard, P., Monroy-Hernández, A., & Savage, S. (2015). Political Bots and the Manipulation of Public Opinion in Venezuela. *ArXiv:1507.07109 [Physics]*. http://arxiv.org/abs/1507.07109

Fowler, Y. R. & Goodman, C. (2017, June 22). Opinion | How Tinder Could Take Back the White House. *New York Times*. https://www.nytimes.com/2017/06/22/opinion/how-tinder-could-take-back-the-white-house.html

François, C. (2019). Actors, Behaviors, Content: A Disinformation ABC. *Transatlantic High Level Working Group on Content Moderation Online and Freedom of Expression*, 10.

Frystyk, H. (1994, July). *The Internet Protocol Stack*. https://www.w3.org/People/Frystyk/thesis/TcpIp.html

Fundamedios (2015, October 7). *Tres medios digitales sufren ataques tras publicar información sobre Hacking Team* – [Three Digital Media Outlets Attacked after Publishing Information about Hacking Team]. http://web.archive.org/web/20151002221332/https://www.fundamedios.org/alertas/tres-medios-digitales-sufren-ataques-tras-publicar-informacion-sobre-hacking-team/

Gallagher, E. (2015, August 14). Mexican Botnet Dirty Wars. /v/camp2015-6795-mexican_botnet_dirty_wars

Gayed, J. (2019, April 25). How Building a Slack Bot Helped Us Send News Notifications. *NYT Open*. https://open.nytimes.com/how-building-a-slack-bot-helped-us-send-news-notifications-f28c681a5b3b

Gehl, R. W. (2018). *Weaving the Dark Web Legitimacy on Freenet, Tor, and I2P*. MIT Press.

Geiger, R. S. (2014). Bots, Bespoke Code, and the Materiality of Software Platforms. *Information, Communication & Society*, 17(3), 342–356.

Geiger, R. S. (2018). The Lives of Bots. *ArXiv:1810.09590 [Cs]*. http://arxiv.org/abs/1810.09590

Gillespie, T. (2012). Can an Algorithm Be Wrong? *Limn*, 1(2). http://escholarship.org/uc/item/0jk9k4hj

Glassman, M. (2020, August 27). Video Game Numbers Show an Industry's All-Out Growth. *Bloomberg Businessweek*. https://www.bloomberg.com/news/articles/2020-08-27/this-is-the-video-game-industry-s-coronavirus-pandemic-boom-in-charts

Gleicher, N. (2018, December 6). Coordinated Inauthentic Behavior Explained. *About Facebook*. https://about.fb.com/news/2018/12/inside-feed-coordinated-inauthentic-behavior/

Google (2020a). Googlebot | Google Search Central. *Google Developers*. https://developers.google.com/search/docs/advanced/crawling/googlebot

Google (2020b). How Google Search Works | Google Search Central. *Google Developers*. https://developers.google.com/search/docs/beginner/how-search-works

Gorwa, R. (2017a). Computational Propaganda in Poland: False Amplifiers and the Digital Public Sphere. Oxford Internet Institute, 32.

Gorwa, R. (2017b, October 23). Twitter Has a Serious Bot Problem and Wikipedia Might Have the Solution. Quartz. https://qz.com/1108092/twitter-has-a-serious-bot-problem-and-wikipedia-might-have-the-solution/

Gorwa, R. & Guilbeault, D. (2018). Unpacking the Social Media Bot: A Typology to Guide Research and Policy. *Policy & Internet*, 12(2), 225–248. https://doi.org/10.1002/poi3.184

GPT-3 (2020, September 8). A Robot Wrote this Entire Article. Are You Scared Yet, Human? | *GPT-3*. Guardian. http://www.theguardian.com/commentisfree/2020/sep/08/robot-wrote-this-article-gpt-3

Graham, L. (2016, March 30). Tay, Microsoft's AI Program, Is Back Online. *CNBC*. https://www.cnbc.com/2016/03/30/tay-microsofts-ai-program-is-back-online.html

Gray, J., Srinet, K., Jernite, Y., Yu, H., Chen, Z., Guo, D., Goyal, S., Zitnick, C. L., & Szlam, A. (2019). CraftAssist: A Framework for Dialogue-Enabled Interactive Agents. Facebook AI. https://www.minecraftbot.com/

Griffith, E. & Simonite, T. (2018, January 8). Facebook's Virtual Assistant M Is Dead. So Are Chatbots. *Wired*. https://www.wired.com/story/facebooks-virtual-assistant-m-is-dead-so-are-chatbots/

Grimme, C., Preuss, M., Adam, L., & Trautmann, H. (2017). Social Bots: Human-Like by Means of Human Control? *ArXiv:1706.07624 [Cs]*. http://arxiv.org/abs/1706.07624

Grossman, W. M. (1995, December 1). Alt.scientology.war. *Wired*. https://www.wired.com/1995/12/alt-scientology-war/

Gudivada, V. N., Raghavan, V. V., Grosky, W. I., & Kasanagottu, R. (1997). Information Retrieval on the World Wide Web. *IEEE Internet Computing*, 1(5), 56–68.

Guglielmi, G. (2020). The Next-Generation Bots Interfering with the US Election. *Nature*, 587(7832), 21–21. https://doi.org/10.1038/d41586-020-03034-5

Guilbeault, D. (2016). Growing Bot Security: An Ecological View of Bot Agency. *The International Journal of Communication*, 10, 5003–5021.

Gunkel, D. J. (2012). *The Machine Question: Critical Perspectives on AI, Robots, and Ethics*. MIT Press.

Guo, E. (2021, June 24). How YouTube's Rules Are Used to Silence Human Rights Activists. *MIT Technology Review*. https://www.technologyreview.com/2021/06/24/1027048/youtube-xinjiang-censorship-human-rights-atajurt/

Guzman, A. (ed.). (2018). *Human–Machine Communication: Rethinking Communication, Technology, and Ourselves*. Peter Lang Publishing. https://doi.org/10.3726/b14399

Guzman, A. L. & Lewis, S. C. (2020). Artificial Intelligence and Communication: A Human–Machine Communication Research Agenda. *New Media & Society*, 22(1), 70–86. https://doi.org/10.1177/1461444819858691

Hall, D. (2019, December 10). The ELIZA Effect. *99% Invisible*. https://99percentinvisible.org/episode/the-eliza-effect/

Hao, K. (2020, August 14). A College Kid Created a Fake, AI-Generated Blog. It Reached #1 on Hacker News. *MIT Technology Review*. https://www.technologyreview.com/2020/08/14/1006780/ai-gpt-3-fake-blog-reached-top-of-hacker-news/

Haraway, D. (1991). *Simians, Cyborgs, and Women: The Reinvention of Nature*. Routledge: Taylor and Francis Group. https://www.routledge.com/Simians-Cyborgs-and-Women-The-Reinvention-of-Nature/Haraway/p/book/9780415903875

Hayati, P., Chai, K., Potdar, V., & Talevski, A. (2009). HoneySpam 2.0: Profiling Web Spambot Behaviour. *PRIMA*. https://doi.org/10.1007/978-3-642-11161-7_23

Hegelich, S. & Janetzko, D. (2016). Are Social Bots on Twitter Political Actors? Empirical Evidence from a Ukrainian Social Botnet. *Proceedings of the International AAAI Conference on Web and Social Media*, 10(1), Article 1. https://ojs.aaai.org/index.php/ICWSM/article/view/14764

Hepp, A. (2020). Artificial Companions, Social Bots and Work Bots: Communicative Robots as Research Objects of Media and Communication Studies. *Media, Culture & Society*, 42(7–8), 1410–1426. https://doi.org/10.1177/0163443720916412

Herman, E. & Chomsky, N. (2002). *Manufacturing Consent: The Political Economy of the Mass Media*. Pantheon Books.

Hern, A. (2015, February 12). Randomly Generated Tweet by Bot Prompts Investigation by Dutch police. *Guardian*. http://www.theguardian.com/technology/2015/feb/12/randomly-generated-tweet-by-bot-investigation-dutch-police

Hess, A. (2016, December 14). On Twitter, a Battle Among Political Bots. *New York Times*. http://www.nytimes.com/2016/12/14/arts/on-twitter-a-battle-among-political-bots.html

Hill, K. (2015, February 11). After Twitter Bot Makes Death Threat, its Owner gets Questioned by Police. *Splinter*. https://splinternews.com/after-twitter-bot-makes-death-threat-its-owner-gets-qu-1793845332

Hill, K. (2020, January 18). The Secretive Company That Might End Privacy as We Know It. *New York Times*. https://www.nytimes.com/2020/01/18/technology/clearview-privacy-facial-recognition.html

Hofstadter, D. (1995). *Fluid Concepts and Creative Analogies: Computer Models of the Fundamental Mechanisms of Thought*. Basic Books.

Howard, P. N., Ganesh, B., Liotsiou, D., Kelly, J., & François, C. (2018). The IRA, Social Media and Political Polarization in the United

States, 2012–2018. *Computational Propaganda Research Project.* http://comprop.oii.ox.ac.uk/wp-content/uploads/sites/93/2018/12/IRA-Report-2018.pdf

Howard, P. N. & Kollanyi, B. (2016). Bots, #StrongerIn, and #Brexit: Computational Propaganda during the UK–EU Referendum. *ArXiv:1606.06356 [Physics].* http://arxiv.org/abs/1606.06356

Howard, P. N. & Parks, M. R. (2012). Social Media and Political Change: Capacity, Constraint, and Consequence. *Journal of Communication,* 62(2), 359–362. https://doi.org/10.1111/j.1460-2466.2012.01626.x

Howard, P. N., Woolley, S., & Calo, R. (2018). Algorithms, Bots, and Political Communication in the US 2016 Election: The Challenge of Automated Political Communication for Election Law and Administration. *Journal of Information Technology & Politics,* 15(2), 81–93. https://doi.org/10.1080/19331681.2018.1448735

Hughes, M. (2019, April 17). Bots Drove nearly 40% of Internet Traffic Last Year – And the Naughty Ones Are Getting Smarter. *The Next Web.* https://thenextweb.com/security/2019/04/17/bots-drove-nearly-40-of-internet-traffic-last-year-and-the-naughty-ones-are-getting-smarter/

Hürriyet Daily News (2014, July 31). Turkey takes Record for Removal Requests from Twitter – *Turkey News.* https://www.hurriyetdailynews.com/turkey-takes-record-for-removal-requests-from-twitter-69843

Hürriyet Daily News (2017, September 20). Turkey Top Country Seeking Removal of Content on Twitter: Report. *Hürriyet Daily News.* https://www.hurriyetdailynews.com/turkey-top-country-seeking-removal-of-content-on-twitter-report-118172

Hutchins, J. (2003). ALPAC: The (In)Famous Report. *Readings in Machine Translation,* 131–136.

Hwang, T. (2018). Computational Power and the Social Impact of Artificial Intelligence (SSRN Scholarly Paper ID 3147971). *Social Science Research Network.* https://doi.org/10.2139/ssrn.3147971

Hwang, T., Pearce, I., & Nanis, M. (2012). Socialbots: Voices from the Fronts. *Interactions,* 19(2), 38–45.

Imperva (2020). Bad Bot Report Bad Bots Strike Back. https://www.imperva.com/resources/reports/Imperva_BadBot_Report_V2.0.pdf

Indiana University Center for Complex Networks and Systems Research (2011). Profile of the 2012 Presidential Candidates' Twitter Followers. *CNetS.* https://cnets.indiana.edu/groups/nan/truthy/statistical-profile-of-the-2012-presidential-candidates-twitter-followers/

Indiana University Knowledge Base (2020, August 5). Web Search Robots. https://kb.iu.edu/d/aeub

Iovine, A. (2020, January 31). Inside the Future of Online Dating: AI Swiping and Concierge Bots. *Mashable*. https://mashable.com/article/tinder-hack-bot-ai-dating/

Isaacson, W. (2014). *The Innovators*. Simon & Schuster.

Jack, C. (2017). Lexicon of Lies: Terms for Problematic Information. *Data & Society*. https://datasociety.net/output/lexicon-of-lies/

Johnson, K. (2016, August 17). The Bot that Beat 170,000 Tickets Launches in Seattle Next Week, then San Francisco. *VentureBeat*. https://venturebeat.com/2016/08/17/the-bot-that-beat-170000-parking-tickets-launches-in-seattle-next-week-san-francisco-next/

Julia's Home Page (1994, July 10). http://www.lazytoad.com/lti/julia/

Jurafsky, D. & Martin, J. H. (2018). *Speech and Language Processing: An Introduction to Natural Language Processing, Computational Linguistics, and Speech Recognition* (3rd edn. draft). https://web.stanford.edu/~jurafsky/slp3/edbook_oct162019.pdf

Jurafsky, D. & Martin, J. H. (2020). *Chapter 24 Chatbots & Dialogue Systems (from Speech and Language Processing)*. https://web.stanford.edu/~jurafsky/slp3/24.pdf

Kasperkevic, J. (2015, April 22). Swiss police release robot that bought ecstasy online. *Guardian*. http://www.theguardian.com/world/2015/apr/22/swiss-police-release-robot-random-darknet-shopper-ecstasy-deep-web

Kazemi, D. (2018, May 17). US grocer LeBron James's online delivery deal sends Ocado shares rocketing [Microblog]. *Twitter @TwoHeadlines*. https://twitter.com/TwoHeadlines/status/997131650348744704

Keefe, J., Thaker, A., & Kopf, D. (2019, May 16). Follow Indian politics with Quartz's Twitter bot. *Quartz India*. https://qz.com/india/1620249/introducing-the-india-political-watch-bot-on-twitter/

Keelan, J., Pavri, V., Balakrishnan, R., & Wilson, K. (2010). An analysis of the Human Papilloma Virus vaccine debate on MySpace blogs. *Vaccine*, 28(6), 1535–1540. https://doi.org/10.1016/j.vaccine.2009.11.060

Kelleher, J. & Tierney, B. (2018). *Data Science*. MIT Press.

Keller, F. B., Schoch, D., Stier, S., & Yang, J. (2020). Political Astroturfing on Twitter: How to Coordinate a Disinformation Campaign. *Political Communication*, 37(2), 256–280. https://doi.org/10.1080/10584609.2019.1661888

Keller, M. (2015, April 1). Mockingjay: A Smarter Repeater. *Source*. https://source.opennews.org/articles/mockingjay/

Kennedy, K. (2009). Textual Machinery: Authorial Agency and Bot-Written Texts in Wikipedia. In M. Smith & B. Warnick (eds.),

The Responsibilities of Rhetoric: Proceedings of the 2008 Rhetoric Society of America Conference. Waveland Press.

Kiehl, C. (2012, March 23). *How to Build a Python Bot That Can Play Web Games.* Code Envato Tuts+. https://code.tutsplus.com/tutorials/how-to-build-a-python-bot-that-can-play-web-games-active-11117

King, G., Pan, J., & Roberts, M. E. (2017). How the Chinese Government Fabricates Social Media Posts for Strategic Distraction, not Engaged Argument. *American Political Science Review, 111*(3), 484–501.

Kolakowski, M. (2019, June 25). *How Robots Rule the Stock Market.* Investopedia. https://www.investopedia.com/news/how-robots-rule-stock-market-spx-djia/

Kollanyi, B. (2016). Automation, Algorithms, and Politics| Where Do Bots Come From? An Analysis of Bot Codes Shared on GitHub. *International Journal of Communication, 10*(0), 20.

Kollanyi, B., Howard, P. N., & Woolley, S. (2016). Bots and Automation over Twitter during the US Election. *Project on Computational Propaganda.* http://blogs.oii.ox.ac.uk/politicalbots/wp-content/uploads/sites/89/2016/11/Data-Memo-US-Election.pdf

Kono, T. (2013). Extended Mind and After: Socially Extended Mind and Actor-Network. *Integrative Psychological and Behavioral Science, 48*(1), 48–60.

Koster, M. (n.d.). *Database of Web Robots, Overview.* Retrieved November 13, 2020, from http://webdoc.sub.gwdg.de/ebook/aw/1999/webcrawler/mak/projects/robots/active/html/index.html

Koster, M. (1994, June 30). *A Standard for Robot Exclusion.* http://www.robotstxt.org/orig.html

Koster, M. (1996, December 4). IETF Network Working Group, Internet Draft. https://www.robotstxt.org/norobots-rfc.txt

Krebs, B. (2012, March 12). Twitter Bots Target Tibetan Protests. *Krebs on Security.* https://krebsonsecurity.com/2012/03/twitter-bots-target-tibetan-protests/

Kung W. (2018a, September 26). *Shei dai fengxiang: Bei jinqian caonong de gonggong yulun zhanzheng* [Who's Driving Public Opinion: The Public Opinion War Being Manipulated by Money]. *The Reporter.* https://www.twreporter.org/a/disinformation-manufacturing-consent-the-political-economy

Kung W. (2018b, September 26). *Wang hong, jia zhanghao, suren anzhuang – Zhide xinlai de koubai xingxiao* [Internet Celebrities, Fake Accounts, regular people's dark pile – Trustworthy marketing companies?]. https://www.twreporter.org/a/disinformation-manufacturing-consent-mom

References

Kushner, D. (2005, September 1). On the Internet, Nobody Knows You're a Bot. *Wired*. https://www.wired.com/2005/09/pokerbots/

LaFrance, A. (2017, January 31). The Internet Is Mostly Bots. *The Atlantic*. https://www.theatlantic.com/technology/archive/2017/01/bots-bots-bots/515043/

Lamo, M. & Calo, R. (2018). Regulating Bot Speech (SSRN Scholarly Paper ID 3214572). *Social Science Research Network*. https://papers.ssrn.com/abstract=3214572

Latour, B. (2007). *Reassembling the Social: An Introduction to Actor-Network-Theory*. Oxford University Press.

Latour, B. (2011). Network Theory| Networks, Societies, Spheres: Reflections of an Actor-network Theorist. *International Journal of Communication*, 5(0), 15.

Law, J. & Hassard, J. (1999). *Actor Network Theory and After* (1st edn.). Wiley-Blackwell.

Lee, E., Woo, J., Kim, H., Mohaisen, A., & Kim, H. K. (2016). You are a Game Bot!: Uncovering Game Bots in MMORPGs via Self-Similarity in the Wild. *Proceedings 2016 Network and Distributed System Security Symposium*. Network and Distributed System Security Symposium, San Diego, CA. https://doi.org/10.14722/ndss.2016.23436

Lee, P. (2016, March 25). Learning from Tay's Introduction. *The Official Microsoft Blog*. https://blogs.microsoft.com/blog/2016/03/25/learning-tays-introduction/

Lee, S. (2018, July 20). Venmo a Friend about "drugs" or "Sex" and this Twitter Bot Will Rat You Out. *Mercury News*. https://www.mercurynews.com/2018/07/20/venmo-a-friend-about-drugs-or-sex-and-this-twitter-bot-will-rat-you-out/

Lefkowitz, M. (2019, September 25). *Professor's Perceptron Paved the Way for AI – 60 Years Too Soon*. Cornell Chronicle. https://news.cornell.edu/stories/2019/09/professors-perceptron-paved-way-ai-60-years-too-soon

Leonard, A. (1996, April 1). Bots Are Hot! *Wired*. https://www.wired.com/1996/04/netbots/

Leonard, A. (1997). Bots: The Origin of New Species. *HardWired*.

Lewis, S. C., Guzman, A. L., & Schmidt, T. R. (2019). Automation, Journalism, and Human–Machine Communication: Rethinking Roles and Relationships of Humans and Machines in News. *Digital Journalism*, 7(4), 409–427. https://doi.org/10.1080/21670811.2019.1577147

Lewis, S. C., Sanders, A. K., & Carmody, C. (2019). Libel by Algorithm? Automated Journalism and the Threat of Legal Liability. *Journalism*

& *Mass Communication Quarterly*, 96(1), 60–81. https://doi. org/10.1177/1077699018755983

Lewis-Kraus, G. (2016, December 14). The Great A.I. Awakening. *New York Times*. https://www.nytimes.com/2016/12/14/magazine/the-great-ai-awakening.html

Lighthill, J. (1972). *Artificial Intelligence: A General Survey*. http://www.chilton-computing.org.uk/inf/literature/reports/lighthill_report/p001.htm

Liu J. C. H. (2019, December 25). Zhuanfang zhengzhi guwen gongsi Autopolitic chuangbanren du yuan fu shuchu taiwan zhengtan shengxuang fangchengshi, ta dao dongnanya maicelve: Wo shi ceshi minzhu de bingdu [Exclusive interview with founder of political consulting company Autopolitic Du Yuanfu. Exporting the equation of how to win an election, he travels to southeast asia to "sell strategies": I'm testing democracy's viruses]. https://www.twreporter.org/a/information-warfare-business-interview-autopolitic-roger-do

Live Bitcoin News (2018, August 14). A Boost for Businesses and AI Growth as hCaptcha Launches in China. https://www.livebitcoinnews.com/boost-for-businesses-and-ai-growth-as-hcaptcha-launches-in-china/

Lokot, T. & Diakopoulos, N. (2015). News Bots: Automating News and Information Dissemination on Twitter. *Digital Journalism*, 1–18. https://doi.org/10.1080/21670811.2015.1081822

Lokot, T. & Diakopoulos, N. (2016). News Bots. *Digital Journalism*, 4(6), 682–699. https://doi.org/10.1080/21670811.2015.1081822

Long, K., Vines, J., Sutton, S., Brooker, P., Feltwell, T., Kirman, B., Barnett, J., & Lawson, S. (2017). "Could You Define That in Bot Terms"? Requesting, Creating and Using Bots on Reddit. *Proceedings of the 2017 CHI Conference on Human Factors in Computing Systems*, 3488–3500. https://doi.org/10.1145/3025453.3025830

Lugrin, B., Prendinger, H., Andre, E., & Ishizuka, M. (2008). Creating and Scripting Second Life Bots Using MPML3D. 492–493. https://doi.org/10.1007/978-3-540-85483-8_58

Luhn, A. (2015, May 12). Boris Nemtsov Report on Ukraine to be Released by Dead Politician's Allies. *Guardian*. https://www.theguardian.com/world/2015/may/12/boris-nemtsov-report-on-ukraine-to-be-released-by-dead-politicians-allies

Luke, A. (2018). Digital Ethics Now. *Language and Literacy*, 20(3), 185–198. https://doi.org/10.20360/langandlit29416

Mac, R., Haskins, C., & McDonald, L. (2020, February 27). Clearview's Facial Recognition App Has Been Used By The Justice Department, ICE, Macy's, Walmart, And The NBA.

BuzzFeed News. https://www.buzzfeednews.com/article/ryanmac/clearview-ai-fbi-ice-global-law-enforcement

McCullough, W. & Pitts, W. (1943). A Logical Calculus of the Ideas Immanent in Neuron Activity. *Bulletin of Mathematical Biophysics*, 5, 115–133.

McCurry, J. (2017, August 4). South Korea Spy Agency Admits Trying to Rig 2012 Presidential Election. *Guardian.* http://www.theguardian.com/world/2017/aug/04/south-koreas-spy-agency-admits-trying-rig-election-national-intelligence-service-2012

McKelvey, F. (2018). *Internet Daemons: Digital Communications Possessed.* University of Minnesota Press.

McKelvey, F. & Dubois, E. (2017). Computational Propaganda in Canada: The Use of Political Bots. *Project on Computational Propaganda*, Working Paper 2017.6, 32.

MacKenzie, D. (2008). *An Engine, Not a Camera: How Financial Models Shape Markets* (1st edn.). MIT Press.

Maes, P. (1994). Agents That Reduce Work and Information Overload. *Communications of the ACM*, 37(7), 30–40. https://doi.org/10.1145/176789.176792

Magueresse, A., Carles, V., & Heetderks, E. (2020). Low-Resource Languages: A Review of Past Work and Future Challenges. *ArXiv:2006.07264 [Cs].* http://arxiv.org/abs/2006.07264

Mannes, J. (2019, July 12). DoNotPay Launches 1,000 New Bots to Help You with Your Legal Problems. *TechCrunch.* http://social.techcrunch.com/2017/07/12/donotpay-launches-1000-new-bots-to-help-you-with-your-legal-problems/

Marcus, G. (2014, June 9). What Comes After the Turing Test? *The New Yorker.* https://www.newyorker.com/tech/annals-of-technology/what-comes-after-the-turing-test

Marie del Prado, G. (2015). Researchers Say the Turing Test is Almost Worthless. *Business Insider.* https://www.businessinsider.com/ai-researchers-arent-trying-to-pass-the-turing-test-2015-8

Markoff, J. (2008, August 12). Before the Gunfire, Cyberattacks. *New York Times.* https://www.nytimes.com/2008/08/13/technology/13cyber.html

Markoff, J. (2009, March 28). Vast Spy System Loots Computers in 103 Countries. *New York Times.* https://www.nytimes.com/2009/03/29/technology/29spy.html

Markoff, J. (2015). *Machines of Loving Grace: The Quest for Common Ground between Humans and Robots.* Ecco.

Markov, A. (1913). Essai d'une recherche statistique sur le texte du roman "Eugene Onegin" illustrant la liaison des épreuves en chain ("Example of a statistical investigation of the text of "Eugene Onegin" illustrating the dependence between samples in chain"). *Izvistia Imperatorskoi Akademii Nauk (Bulletin de l'Académie Impériale Des Sciences de St Pétersbourg)*, 7, 153–162.

Massanari, A. (2016). *Contested Play: The Culture and Politics of Reddit Bots*. Routledge.

Maus, G. (2017). A Typology of Socialbots (Abbrev.). *Proceedings of the 2017 ACM on Web Science Conference*, 399–400. https://doi.org/10.1145/3091478.3098860

Merrill, J. B. (2020, January 22). Exposing Alleged Corruption with Universal Sentence Encoder and Annoy. Quartz AI Studio. https://qz.ai/exposing-alleged-corruption-with-universal-sentence-encoder-and-annoy/

Metz, C. (2020, November 24). Meet GPT-3. It Has Learned to Code (and Blog and Argue). *New York Times*. https://www.nytimes.com/2020/11/24/science/artificial-intelligence-ai-gpt3.html

Microsoft. (2016a). *TayTweets (@TayandYou) on Twitter*. Twitter. https://twitter.com/TayandYou

Microsoft (2016b). *Zo (@zochats) / Twitter*. Twitter. https://twitter.com/zochats

Miller, C. (2007). What Can Automation Tell Us About Agency? *Rhetoric Society Quarterly*, 37(2), 137–157. https://doi.org/10.1080/02773940601021197

Mims, C. (2010, November 2). Chatbot Wears Down Proponents of Anti-Science Nonsense. *MIT Technology Review*. https://www.technologyreview.com/2010/11/02/261287/chatbot-wears-down-proponents-of-anti-science-nonsense/

Mims, C. (2014, July 27). Advertising's New Frontier: Talk to the Bot. *Wall Street Journal*. https://online.wsj.com/articles/advertisings-new-frontier-talk-to-the-bot-1406493740

Mims, C. (2017, November 12). Without Humans, Artificial Intelligence Is Still Pretty Stupid. *Wall Street Journal*. https://www.wsj.com/articles/without-humans-artificial-intelligence-is-still-pretty-stupid-1510488000

Monaco, N. (2017). Computational Propaganda in Taiwan: Where Digital Democracy Meets Automated Autocracy. *Project on Computational Propaganda*, 32.

Monaco, N. (2019a, November 23). Welcome to the Party: A Data Analysis of Chinese Information Operations CN. *Medium*. https://medium.com/digintel/welcome-to-the-party-a-data-analysis-of-chinese-information-operations-6d48ee186939

Monaco, N. (2019b, November 29). #DemDebates Data: Hashtag

Hijacking, Antivax Disinfo, Cyborgs and Godmen. *Medium*. https://medium.com/digintel/demdebates-data-hashtag-hijacking-antivax-disinfo-cyborgs-and-godmen-44818dea089d

Monaco, N. & Arnaudo, D. (2020, May 28). Data Analytics for Social Media Monitoring. National Democratic Institute. https://www.ndi.org/publications/data-analytics-social-media-monitoring

Monaco, N. & Nyst, C. (2018, July). State-Sponsored Trolling: How Governments Are Deploying Disinformation as Part of Broader Digital Harassment Campaigns. Institute for the Future. http://www.iftf.org/statesponsoredtrolling

Monaco, N., Smith, M., & Studdart, A. (2020, August). Detecting Digital Fingerprints: Tracing Chinese Disinformation in Taiwan. Institute for the Future. https://www.iftf.org/disinfo-in-taiwan

Monaco, N. & Woolley, S. (2017, November 13). Reactions & Regulation in the Age of Computational Propaganda. *The Ripon Society*. http://www.riponsociety.org/article/reactions-regulation-in-the-age-of-computational-propaganda/

Monaco, N. & Woolley, S. (2019). Natural Language Processing and Global Development: A Future-Focused Primer. Framing paper for Convening, University of Texas at Austin. https://www.rtachesn.org/wp-content/uploads/2019/09/Framing-papers_Combined-final.pdf

Moor, J. H. (2003). Turing Test. In *Encyclopedia of Computer Science* (pp. 1801–1802). John Wiley and Sons Ltd.

Morales, E. (2020, November 24). The State of Instagram Bots in 2020 & the Most Effective Bot Companies Right Now. *Medium*. https://medium.com/better-marketing/the-state-of-instagram-bots-in-2020-eb03fd7de30

Morozov, E. (2010). Think Again: The Internet. *Foreign Policy*. https://foreignpolicy.com/2010/04/26/think-again-the-internet/

Mottet, J. (2019, June 20). Let's Create an Instagram Bot to Show You the Power of Selenium! *Medium*. https://medium.com/better-programming/lets-create-an-instagram-bot-to-show-you-the-power-of-selenium-349d7a6744f7

Mozilla (2017, June 6). New Mozilla Poll: Americans from Both Political Parties Overwhelmingly Support Net Neutrality. The Mozilla Blog. https://blog.mozilla.org/blog/2017/06/06/new-mozilla-poll-americans-political-parties-overwhelmingly-support-net-neutrality

Müller, P. (2019, April 23). Winning Against Bots: How Gaming Apps Can Fight Back. *VentureBeat*. https://venturebeat.com/2019/04/23/winning-against-bots-how-gaming-apps-can-fight-back/

Munger, K., Bonneau, R., Nagler, J., & Tucker, J. A. (2019). Elites

Tweet to Get Feet Off the Streets: Measuring Regime Social Media Strategies During Protest. *Political Science Research and Methods*, 7(4), 815–834. https://doi.org/10.1017/psrm.2018.3

Myers, A. (2017, November 30). Artificial Intelligence Index Tracks Emerging Field. *Stanford News*. https://news.stanford.edu/2017/11/30/artificial-intelligence-index-tracks-emerging-field/

Nardi, B. (1995). Studying Context: A Comparison of Activity Theory, Situated action Models, and Distributed Cognition. In *Context and Consciousness: Activity Theory and Human–Computer Interaction* (pp. 69–96). MIT Press.

Neff, G. & Nagy, P. (2016a). Talking to Bots: Symbiotic Agency and the Case of Tay. *International Journal of Communication*, 10(Special Issue), 20.

Neff, G. & Nagy, P. (2016b). Automation, Algorithms, and Politics| Talking to Bots: Symbiotic Agency and the Case of Tay. *International Journal of Communication*, 10(0), 17.

Nemtsov, B. & Bremmer, I. (2000, January 5). Opinion | Russia's Best Bet (Published 2000). *New York Times*. https://www.nytimes.com/2000/01/05/opinion/russia-s-best-bet.html

Neudert, L.-M. (2018, August 22). Future Elections May be Swayed by Intelligent, Weaponized Chatbots. *MIT Technology Review*. https://www.technologyreview.com/2018/08/22/104087/future-elections-may-be-swayed-by-intelligent-weaponized-chatbots/

New York Times (1958, July 8). New Navy Device Learns By Doing; Psychologist Shows Embryo of Computer Designed to Read and Grow Wiser. https://www.nytimes.com/1958/07/08/archives/new-navy-device-learns-by-doing-psychologist-shows-embryo-of.html

Newitz, A. (2015, August 26). Almost None of the Women in the Ashley Madison Database Ever Used the Site [Updated]. *Gizmodo*. https://gizmodo.com/almost-none-of-the-women-in-the-ashley-madison-database-1725558944

Nguyen, M.-H. (2020, January 28). How Customer Service Chatbots and Virtual Assistant Bots Are Providing Key Customer Support Functions. *Business Insider*. https://www.businessinsider.com/customer-service-support-chatbots

Nimmo, B., Eib, C. S., Tamora, L., Johnson, K., Smith, I., Buziashvili, E., Kann, A., Karan, K., Rosas, E. P. de L., & Rizzuto, M. (2019, December 20). #OperationFFS: Fake Face Swarm. https://graphika.com/reports/operationffs-fake-face-swarm/

Noble, S. (2018). *Algorithms of Oppression: How Search Engines Reinforce Racism*. New York University Press.

Oberquelle, H., Kupka, I., & Maass, S. (1983). A View of Human–Machine Communication and Co-operation. *International Journal of Man–Machine Studies*, 19(4), 309–333. https://doi.org/10.1016/S0020-7373(83)80057-1

O'Brien, F. (2020, October 7). Developing for the Semantic Web. *Smashing Magazine.* https://www.smashingmagazine.com/2020/10/developing-semantic-web/

Office of the Director of National Intelligence (ODNI) (2021). Assessing the Saudi Government's Role in the Killing of Jamal Khashoggi. http://web.archive.org/web/20210226180954/https://www.odni.gov/files/ODNI/documents/assessments/Assessment-Saudi-Gov-Role-in-JK-Death-20210226.pdf

Ohno, J. (2018, February 8). How Bots Were Born From Spam. *Medium.* https://enkiv2.medium.com/how-bots-were-born-from-spam-62f6c621351f

Olanaff, D. & Constine, J. (2015, August 26). Facebook Is Adding a Personal Assistant Called "M" to Your Messenger App. *TechCrunch.* https://social.techcrunch.com/2015/08/26/facebook-is-adding-a-personal-assistant-called-m-to-your-messenger-app/

Online Etymology Dictionary (n.d.). *Origin and Meaning of Robot.* https://www.etymonline.com/word/robot

O'Reilly, T. (2005, September 30). *What Is Web 2.0?* https://oreilly.com{file}

Osborne, C. (2019, April 17). Bad Bots Now Make Up 20 Percent of Web Traffic. ZDNet. https://www.zdnet.com/article/bad-bots-focus-on-financial-targets-make-up-20-percent-of-web-traffic/

Park, A. & Wang, J. (2020). Did Trading Bots Resurrect the CAPM? (SSRN Scholarly Paper ID 3515635). *Social Science Research Network.* https://doi.org/10.2139/ssrn.3515635

Parrish, A. (2015). *@everyword: The Book.* Instar Books. https://www.instarbooks.com/books/everyword.html

Parrish, A. (2016, February 26). Bots: A Definition and Some Historical Threads. *Points: Data and Society.* https://points.datasociety.net/bots-a-definition-and-some-historical-threads-47738c8ab1ce

Peiser, J. (2019, February 5). The Rise of the Robot Reporter. *New York Times.* https://www.nytimes.com/2019/02/05/business/media/artificial-intelligence-journalism-robots.html

Phan, T. T. (2021, January 10). Why Genies Partnered with Unity to Build its 3D Avatar World. *The Hustle.* https://thehustle.co/why-genies-partnered-with-unity-to-build-its-3d-avatar-world/

Pierce, J. & Carroll, J. (1966). Language and Machines: Computers in Translation and Linguistics. Automatic Language Processing

Advisory Committee (ALPAC). http://www.mt-archive.info/ALPAC-1966.pdf
Poibeau, T. (2017). *Machine Translation*. MIT Press.
Pomerantsev, P. (2014). Nothing Is True and Everything Is Possible: The Surreal Heart of the New Russia. *PublicAffairs*.
Pomerantsev, P. (2019). This is Not Propaganda: Adventures in the War against Reality. *PublicAffairs*.
Pomerantz, J. (2015). *Metadata*. MIT Press.
Porr, L. (2020, August 3). My GPT-3 Blog Got 26 Thousand Visitors in 2 Weeks. https://liamp.substack.com/p/my-gpt-3-blog-got-26-thousand-visitors
Poulsen, K. (2019, February 10). Inside the Secret Facebook War for Mormon Hearts and Minds. *The Daily Beast*. https://www.thedailybeast.com/inside-the-secret-facebook-war-for-mormon-hearts-and-minds
Preece, J., Rogers, Y., Sharp, H., Benyon, D., Holland, S., & Carey, T. (1994). *Human–Computer Interaction*. Addison-Wesley Longman Ltd.
Prist, A. (2019, June 10). Conversational AI: How do Chatbots Work? *Medium*. https://medium.com/voiceui/conversational-ai-how-do-chatbots-work-4f1bfd069013
Probyn, A. & Doran, M. (2020, September 13). *China's Mass Surveillance of 35,000 Australians Revealed*. ABC News (Australian Broadcasting Corporation). https://www.abc.net.au/news/2020-09-14/chinese-data-leak-linked-to-military-names-australians/12656668
Qtiesh, A. (2011, April 18). Spam Bots Flooding Twitter to Drown Info About #Syria Protests [Updated]. Global Voices Advocacy. https://advox.globalvoices.org/2011/04/18/spam-bots-flooding-twitter-to-drown-info-about-syria-protests/
Quartz (2020). Quartz AI Studio. https://qz.ai
Rasmussen, T. (2017, June 15). There Was a Tinder Election Bot Fanning the Fire of the Youth Vote. *I-D*. https://i-d.vice.com/en_uk/article/3kd87w/general-election-tinder-bot-youth-vote
Ratkiewicz, J., Conover, M., Meiss, M., Gonçalves, B., Patil, S., Flammini, A., & Menczer, F. (2011). Detecting and Tracking the Spread of Astroturf Memes in Microblog Streams. *Proceedings of the 20th International Conference Companion on World Wide Web – WWW '11*, 249. https://doi.org/10.1145/1963192.1963301
Read, M. (2018, December 26). How Much of the Internet Is Fake? *New York Magazine Intelligencer*. https://nymag.com/intelligencer/2018/12/how-much-of-the-internet-is-fake.html
Reguillo, R. & Maloof, J. R. (2015, May 12). Así es la violencia en

Twitter para censurar a la disidencia en México. *SinEmbargo*. http://www.sinembargo.mx/12-05-2015/1342702

Reilly, J. (2010, October 7). World of Warcraft Reaches 12 Million Subscribers – IGN. *IGN*. https://www.ign.com/articles/2010/10/07/world-of-warcraft-reaches-12-million-subscribers

Reynolds, M. (2016, March 31). Microsoft is Betting that Bots "Are the New Apps." *Wired UK*. https://www.wired.co.uk/article/microsoft-build-bots-ai-cortana-keynote-conference

Ries, B. (2014, December 10). Senate Staffer Tries to Scrub "Torture" Reference from Wikipedia's CIA Torture Article. *Mashable*. https://mashable.com/2014/12/10/senate-wikipedia-torture-report/

Rivera, J. (2020, July 10). How Good Are You at Spotting Bots on Dating Apps? *USA TODAY*. https://www.usatoday.com/story/tech/2020/07/10/dating-app-bots-learn-how-spot-them-before-swiping/5406539002/

Roberts, M. (2020). *Censored: Distraction and Diversion Inside China's Great Firewall*. Princeton University Press.

Roberts, S. (2020, June 16). Who's a Bot? Who's Not? *New York Times*. https://www.nytimes.com/2020/06/16/science/social-media-bots-kazemi.html

Robertson, J., Riley, M., & Willis, A. (2016, March 31). How to Hack an Election. *Bloomberg.Com*. https://www.bloomberg.com/features/2016-how-to-hack-an-election/

Rodríguez-Gómez, R. A., Maciá-Fernández, G., & García-Teodoro, P. (2013). Survey and Taxonomy of Botnet Research Through Life-Cycle. *ACM Computing Surveys*, 45(4), 45:1–45:33. https://doi.org/10.1145/2501654.2501659

Rosenblatt, F. (1958). The Perceptron: A Probabilistic Model for Information Storage and Organization in the Brain. *Psychological Review*, 65(6), 385–407. https://doi.org/10.1037/h0042519

Roth, A. (2018, December 12). "Hi-Tech Robot" at Russia Forum Turns Out to Be Man in Suit. *Guardian*. http://www.theguardian.com/world/2018/dec/12/high-tech-robot-at-russia-forum-turns-out-to-be-man-in-robot-suit

Sample, I. & Hern, A. (2014, June 9). Scientists Dispute Whether Computer "Eugene Goostman" Passed Turing Test. *Guardian*. http://www.theguardian.com/technology/2014/jun/09/scientists-disagree-over-whether-turing-test-has-been-passed

Sanger, D. E. (2019). *The Perfect Weapon: War, Sabotage, and Fear in the Cyber Age*. Crown.

Sang-Hun, C. (2013, November 21). Prosecutors Detail Attempt to Sway South Korean Election. *New York Times*. https://www.nytimes.

com/2013/11/22/world/asia/prosecutors-detail-bid-to-sway-south-korean-election.html

Sang-Hun, C. (2017, August 30). Former South Korean Spy Chief Sentenced for Trying to Sway Election. *New York Times*. https://www.nytimes.com/2017/08/30/world/asia/south-korea-spy-chief-sentenced.html

Sanovich, S. (2017). Computational Propaganda in Russia: The Origins of Digital Misinformation. Oxford Internet Institute. https://www.oii.ox.ac.uk/blog/computational-propaganda-in-russia-the-origins-of-digital-misinformation/

Savage, S., Monroy-Hernandez, A., & Hollerer, T. (2015). Botivist: Calling Volunteers to Action Using Online Bots. https://doi.org/10.1145/2818048.2819985

Sawers, P. (2019, January 29). Alphabet's Jigsaw Expands Project Shield DDoS Protection to European Political Bodies. *VentureBeat*. https://venturebeat.com/2019/01/28/alphabets-jigsaw-expands-project-shield-ddos-protection-to-european-political-bodies/

SCF (2020, July 6). Turkey Made Highest Number of Removal Requests to Twitter in 2019, Report Shows. Stockholm Center for Freedom. https://stockholmcf.org/turkey-made-highest-number-of-removal-requests-to-twitter-in-2019-report-shows/

Schneiderman, B. & Plaisant, C. (2009). *Designing the User Interface: Strategies for Effective Human–Computer Interaction* (5th edn.). Pearson.

Schreckinger, B. (2016, September 30). Inside Trump's "Cyborg" Twitter Army. *Politico*. https://www.politico.com/story/2016/09/donald-trump-twitter-army-228923

Scott-Railton, J., Marczak, B., Razzak, B. A., Crete-Nishihata, M., & Deibert, R. (2017, June 19). Reckless Exploit: Mexican Journalists, Lawyers, and a Child Targeted with NSO Spyware. *The Citizen Lab*. https://citizenlab.ca/2017/06/reckless-exploit-mexico-nso/

Searle, J. R. (1980). Minds, Brains, and Programs. *Behavioral and Brain Sciences*, 3(3), 417–424. https://doi.org/10.1017/S0140525X00005756

Serban, I. V., Lowe, R., Henderson, P., Charlin, L., & Pineau, J. (2017). A Survey of Available Corpora for Building Data-Driven Dialogue Systems. *ArXiv:1512.05742 [Cs, Stat]*. http://arxiv.org/abs/1512.05742

Shachtman, N. (2009, March 11). Kremlin Kids: We Launched the Estonian Cyber War. *Wired*. https://www.wired.com/2009/03/pro-kremlin-gro/

Sharkey, N. (2012, June 20). Alan Turing: The Experiment that Shaped Artificial Intelligence. *BBC News*. https://www.bbc.com/news/technology-18475646

Shepard, A. (2017, September 29). Tay Scandal Taught Us to Take Accountability, Says Microsoft CEO. *IT Pro.* https://www.itpro.com/strategy/29592/tay-scandal-taught-us-to-take-accountability-says-microsoft-ceo

Shuler, R. (2002). How Does the Internet Work? https://web.stanford.edu/class/msande91si/www-spr04/readings/week1/InternetWhitepaper.htm

Silverman, C., Lytvynenko, J., & Kung, W. (2020, January 6). Disinformation for Hire: How a New Breed of PR Firms Is Selling Lies Online. *BuzzFeed News.* https://www.buzzfeednews.com/article/craigsilverman/disinformation-for-hire-black-pr-firms

Singel, R. (2018). Filtering Out the Bots: What Americans Actually Told the FCC about Net Neutrality Repeal. *Stanford Center for Internet and Society (CiS).* https://cyberlaw.stanford.edu/files/blogs/FilteringOutTheBotsUniqueNetNeutralityComments.pdf

Singletary, M. & Shin, Y. (2020, May 22). Ask Your Retirement Questions to Our Michelle Singletary Bot. *Washington Post.* https://www.washingtonpost.com/graphics/2020/business/retirement-planning-bot/

Soldatov, A. & Borogan, I. (2015). The Red Web: The Struggle between Russia's Digital Dictators and the New Online Revolutionaries (First). *PublicAffairs.*

Solon, O. (2016, November 11). Facebook's Fake News: Mark Zuckerberg Rejects "Crazy Idea" that it Swayed Voters. *Guardian.* http://www.theguardian.com/technology/2016/nov/10/facebook-fake-news-us-election-mark-zuckerberg-donald-trump

Spektor, F., Rodriguez, E., Shorey, S., & Fox, S. (2021, June). Discarded Labor: Countervisualities for Representing AI Integration in Essential Work. Conference on Designing Interactive Systems 2021: 406–419.

Spencer, R. (2014, June 4). Creator of @everyword Explains the Life and Death of a Twitter Experiment. *Guardian.* http://www.theguardian.com/culture/2014/jun/04/everyword-twitter-ends-adam-parrish-english-language

Stieglitz, S., Brachten, F., Ross, B., & Jung, A.-K. (2017). Do Social Bots Dream of Electric Sheep? A Categorisation of Social Media Bot Accounts. https://arxiv.org/abs/1710.04044v1

Stoppard, L. (2018, August 3). Inside The Spinner: A Real-Life Inception Project. *Financial Times.* https://www.ft.com/content/944d068c-8a99-11e8-affd-da9960227309

Streams, K. (2012, December 6). Anonymous "Operation Payback" Hackers Convicted for Costly DDoS Attacks. *The Verge.* https://

www.theverge.com/2012/12/6/3735622/anonymous-conviction-christopher-weatherhead-operation-payback

Stukal, D., Sanovich, S., Bonneau, R., & Tucker, J. A. (2017). Detecting Bots on Russian Political Twitter. *Big Data*, 5(4), 310–324. https://doi.org/10.1089/big.2017.0038

Stukal, D., Sanovich, S., Tucker, J. A., & Bonneau, R. (2019). For Whom the Bot Tolls: A Neural Networks Approach to Measuring Political Orientation of Twitter Bots in Russia. *SAGE Open*, 9(2), 2158244019827715. https://doi.org/10.1177/2158244019827715

Stukal, D., Sanovish, S., Tucker, J. A., & Bonneau, R. (2020). *Bots for Autocrats: How Pro-Government Bots Fight Opposition in Russia*. New York University Center for Social Media and Politics. https://sanovich.com/Bots_for_Autocrats_Stukal_Sanovich_Bonneau_Tucker.pdf

Subrahmanian, V. S., Azaria, A., Durst, S., Kagan, V., Galstyan, A., Lerman, K., Zhu, L., Ferrara, E., Flammini, A., Menczer, F., Stevens, A., Dekhtyar, A., Gao, S., Hogg, T., Kooti, F., Liu, Y., Varol, O., Shiralkar, P., Vydiswaran, V., ... Hwang, T. (2016). The DARPA Twitter Bot Challenge. *Computer*, 49(6), 38–46. https://doi.org/10.1109/MC.2016.183

Suchman, L. (2006). *Human–Machine Reconfigurations: Plans and Situated Actions* (2nd edn.). Cambridge University Press.

Sullivan, D. (2020, May 20). *A Reintroduction to Our Knowledge Graph and Knowledge Panels*. Google. https://blog.google/products/search/about-knowledge-graph-and-knowledge-panels/

Summers, E. & Punzalan, R. (2017). Bots, Seeds and People: Web Archives as Infrastructure. *Proceedings of the 2017 ACM Conference on Computer Supported Cooperative Work and Social Computing*, 821–834. https://doi.org/10.1145/2998181.2998345

Sundman, J. (2003, February 27). Artificial Stupidity. *Salon*. https://www.salon.com/2003/02/26/loebner_part_one/

Swamp Ratte (1995, June 4). Statement Concerning the "Church" of Scientology. https://web.archive.org/web/20060316225036/https://www.cultdeadcow.com/news/scientology.txt

Swanstrom, L. (2019, December 15). Climate Bot Panegyric: An Interview with Nigel Leck. https://electronicbookreview.com/essay/climate-bot-panegyric-an-interview-with-nigel-leck/

Sweigart, A. (2015, January 8). Programming a Bot to Play the "Sushi Go Round" Flash Game – The Invent with Python Blog. http://inventwithpython.com/blog/2014/12/17/programming-a-bot-to-play-the-sushi-go-round-flash-game/

Takahashi, D. (2020, October 20). Genies Will Let Consumers Create Their Own 3D Avatars with Giphy and Gucci. *VentureBeat*. https://

venturebeat.com/2020/10/20/genies-will-let-consumers-create-their-own-3d-avatars-with-giphy-and-gucci/

Tarnoff, B. & Weigel, M. (2020). Voices from the Valley Tech Workers Talk About What They Do – And How They Do It. *FSGO / Logic*.

Thomas, K., Grier, C., & Paxson, V. (2012). Adapting Social Spam Infrastructure for Political Censorship. *Proceedings of the 5th USENIX Conference on Large-Scale Exploits and Emergent Threats*, 13.

Thurman, N., Lewis, S. C., & Kunert, J. (2019). Algorithms, Automation, and News. *Digital Journalism*, 7(8), 980–992. https://doi.org/10.1080/21670811.2019.1685395

Toor, A. (2016, October 13). This Twitter Bot is Tracking Dictators' Flights in and out of Geneva. *The Verge*. https://www.theverge.com/2016/10/13/13243072/twitter-bot-tracks-dictator-planes-geneva-gva-tracker

Triquet, F. (2016, September 1). Bots In The Gaming World: What, Who, How And Why? SAP Conversational AI Blog. https://cai.tools.sap/blog/bot-in-video-games/

Tufekci, Z. (2017). *Twitter and Tear Gas: The Power and Fragility of Networked Protest*. Yale University Press.

Turing, A. (1950). Computing Machinery and Intelligence. *Mind*, 49(236), 433–460.

Turner, B. S. (ed.). (2009). Chapter Seven: Actor Network Theory and Material Semiotics. In *The New Blackwell Companion to Social Theory*. Wiley-Blackwell.

Turner, F. (2006). *From Counterculture to Cyberculture*. University of Chicago Press.

United States Cybersecurity & Infrastructure Security Agency (2016, October 17). Heightened DDoS Threat Posed by Mirai and Other Botnets. https://us-cert.cisa.gov/ncas/alerts/TA16-288A

University of Reading (2014, June 8). Turing Test Success Marks Milestone in Computing History. http://www.reading.ac.uk

Veale, T. & Cook, M. (2018). *Twitterbots: Making Machines that Make Meaning* (1st edn.). MIT Press.

Volchek, D. & Sinclair, D. (2015, March 25). One Professional Russian Troll Tells All. RadioFreeEurope/RadioLiberty. https://www.rferl.org/a/how-to-guide-russian-trolling-trolls/26919999.html

Voon, C. (2015, July 17). A Twitter Bot That Generates Beautiful, Imaginary Moths. *Hyperallergic*. https://hyperallergic.com/222029/a-twitter-bot-that-generates-beautiful-imaginary-moths/

Walker, J. (2019, December). Chatbot Comparison – Facebook, Microsoft, Amazon, and Google. *Emerj*. https://emerj.com/ai-sector-overviews/chatbot-comparison-facebook-microsoft-amazon-google/

Warwick, K. & Shah, H. (2016). Can Machines Think? A Report on Turing Test Experiments at the Royal Society. *Journal of Experimental & Theoretical Artificial Intelligence*, 28(6), 989–1007. https://doi.org/10.1080/0952813X.2015.1055826

WashPostPR (2018, March 23). The Post's Heliograf and ModBot Technologies take First Place in 2018 Global BIGGIES Awards. *Washington Post*. https://www.washingtonpost.com/pr/wp/2018/03/23/the-posts-heliograf-and-modbot-technologies-take-first-place-in-2018-global-biggies-awards/

Watts, C. & Hwang, T. (2020, September 10). Opinion | Deepfakes are Coming for American Democracy. Here's How We Can Prepare. *Washington Post*. https://www.washingtonpost.com/opinions/2020/09/10/deepfakes-are-coming-american-democracy-heres-how-we-can-prepare/

Weizenbaum, J. (1966). ELIZA – A Computer Program For the Study of Natural Language Communication Between Man and Machine. *Communications of the ACM*, 9(1), 36–45.

Weizenbaum, J. (1976). *Computer Power and Human Reason: From Judgment to Calculation*. W.H. Freeman and Company.

White, G. L. (2015, March 1). Boris Nemtsov's Career Traces Arc of Russia's Dimmed Hopes for Democracy. *Wall Street Journal*. https://www.wsj.com/articles/boris-nemtsovs-career-traces-arc-of-russias-dimmed-hopes-for-democracy-1425168024

Williams, J. (2018, May 22). Should AI Always Identify Itself? It's More Complicated Than You Might Think. Electronic Frontier Foundation. https://www.eff.org/deeplinks/2018/05/should-ai-always-identify-itself-its-more-complicated-you-might-think

Wilson, J. (2020, January 31). US Neo-Nazi Faces $12.9m Fine for Sending Racist Robocalls. *Guardian*. https://www.theguardian.com/us-news/2020/jan/31/us-fcc-neo-nazi-fine-robocalls

Winner, L. (1980). Do Artifacts Have Politics? *Daedalus*, 109(1), 121–136.

Wolchover, N. (2011, September 7). How the Cleverbot Computer Chats like a Human. NBC News. https://www.nbcnews.com/id/wbna44434584

Wong, J. C. (2019, August 23). Document Reveals how Facebook Downplayed Early Cambridge Analytica Concerns. *Guardian*. https://www.theguardian.com/technology/2019/aug/23/cambridge-analytica-facebook-response-internal-document

Woodford, C. (2005). *The Internet: A Historical Encyclopedia* (vol. 2). ABC-CLIO. https://books.google.com/books?id=qi-ItIG6QLwC&pg=RA2-PA135&lpg=RA2-PA135&dq=usenet+bots&source=bl&ots=

uAOKyrL4EF&sig=ACfU3U3AIDrT4C33ojFBN3K_ekvAzc63MQ&hl=en&sa=X&ved=2ahUKEwiOt5PttoDtAhWJsZ4KHZofAxYQ6AEwD3oECAsQAg#v=onepage&q=usenet%20bots&f=false

Wooldridge, M. (2020). *A Brief History of Artificial Intelligence*. Flatiron Books.

Woolley, S. (2017, April 10). Bots Aren't Just Service Tools – They're a Whole New Form of Media. Quartz. https://qz.com/954255/bots-are-the-newest-form-of-new-media/

Woolley, S. (2018). *Manufacturing Consensus: Computational Propaganda and the 2016 US Presidential Election*. University of Washington.

Woolley, S. (2020a). *The Reality Game: How the Next Wave of Technology Will Break the Truth*. PublicAffairs.

Woolley, S. (2020b). Bots and Computational Propaganda: Automation for Communication and Control. In J. A. Tucker & N. Persily (eds.), *Social Media and Democracy: The State of the Field, Prospects for Reform* (pp. 89–110). Cambridge University Press. https://www.cambridge.org/core/books/social-media-and-democracy/bots-and-computational-propaganda-automation-for-communication-and-control/A15EE25C278B442EF00199AA660BFADD

Woolley, S. & Guilbeault, D. (2016, November 1). How Twitter Bots Are Shaping the Election. *The Atlantic*. https://www.theatlantic.com/technology/archive/2016/11/election-bots/506072/

Woolley, S. & Guilbeault, D. (2017, May). *Computational Propaganda in the United States of America: Manufacturing Consensus Online*. The Computational Propaganda Project. https://comprop.oii.ox.ac.uk/research/working-papers/computational-propaganda-in-the-united-states-of-america-manufacturing-consensus-online/

Woolley, S. & Howard, P. N. (2019). *Computational Propaganda: Political Parties, Politicians, and Political Manipulation on Social Media*. Oxford University Press.

Woolley, S., Pakzad, R., & Monaco, N. (2019, June 21). *Incubating Hate: Islamophobia and Gab*. The German Marshall Fund of the United States. http://www.gmfus.org/publications/incubating-hate-islamophobia-and-gab

Woolley, S. & Howard, P. (2016, May 15). Bots Unite to Automate the Presidential Election. *Wired*. https://www.wired.com/2016/05/twitterbots-2/

Woolley, S. & Hwang, T. (2015, May 14). Bring on the Bots. *Civicist*. https://civichall.org/civicist/bring-on-the-bots/

Woolley, S. & Monaco, N. (2020, July 24). *Amplify the Party, Suppress the Opposition: Social Media, Bots, and Electoral Fraud*. Georgetown Law

Technology Review. https://georgetownlawtechreview.org/amplify-the-party-suppress-the-opposition-social-media-bots-and-electoral-fraud/GLTR-07-2020/

Woolley, S., Shorey, S., & Howard, P. (2018). The Bot Proxy: Designing Automated Self Expression. In *A Networked Self and Platforms, Stories, Connections* (pp. 59–76). Routledge: Taylor and Francis Group. https://doi.org/10.4324/9781315193434-5

Yang, Z., Wilson, C., Wang, X., Gao, T., Zhao, B. Y., & Dai, Y. (2014). Uncovering Social Network Sybils in the Wild. *ACM Transactions on Knowledge Discovery from Data (TKDD)*, 8(1), 1–29.

York, G. (2012, February 1). Buying a Better Image: African Leaders Enlist US Agencies for Pricey Reputation Makeovers. *The Globe and Mail*.

Zadeh, L. A. (1965). Fuzzy Sets. *Information and Control*, 8(3), 338–353. https://doi.org/10.1016/S0019-9958(65)90241-X

Zarka, L. (2018, November 26). The Rise of the Robot Therapist. *Medium*. https://thebolditalic.com/the-rise-of-the-robot-therapist-459b20f770a9

Zegart, A. & Morell, M. (2019, May). Spies, Lies, and Algorithms. *Foreign Affairs*. https://www.foreignaffairs.com/articles/2019-04-16/spies-lies-and-algorithms

Zi, C., Gianvecchio, S., Wang, H., & Jajodia, S. (2010). Who is Tweeting on Twitter: Human, Bot, or Cyborg? *Proceedings of the 26th Annual Computer Security Applications Conference*, 21–30. https://www.eecis.udel.edu/~hnw/paper/acsac10.pdf

Zuboff, S. (2019). *The Age of Surveillance Capitalism: The Fight for a Human Future at the New Frontier of Power* (main edn.). Profile Books.

Zuckerberg, M. (2017, September 27). Facebook Post. Facebook. https://www.facebook.com/zuck/posts/10104067130714241

Index

Aamoth, D., 97, 99
Abokhodair, N., 128–129
ActiveAgent, 18, 25
activity theory, 123, 126
actor network theory (ANT), 39, 123, 127, 129, 133
Adjust, 48
advertising, 15, 18, 19
agency theory, 130, 131–132, 151
Akrich, M., 126–127
@AI_AGW, 76
Albert One, 113
Alexa, 2, 23, 85, 107, 116
Alexander, Lawrence, 53
algorithms
   artificial intelligence, 111, 117
   black box, 146
   bot detection, 26, 80
   finance, 94
   Google, 88
   Jeff_ebooks, 120
   machine learning, 108
   meaning, 58
   misleading information, 53
   objectivity, 44–45
   political bots, 57–59, 61, 148
   Usenet, 11
A.L.I.C.E, 113
ALPAC Report, 105–106
AltaVista, 16, 30
Amazon
   Alexa, 2, 23, 85, 107, 116
   bot technology, 49
   cyberattack, 28
amplification, 23, 59, 64–66, 67, 70, 76

Amplify.ai, 2–3
Ananny, Mi, 45
annoybots, 11, 13
Anonymous, 63
Apple
   bot technology, 49
   Business Chat, 40
   Siri, 2, 23, 49, 85, 87, 107, 116
application programming interfaces (APIs), 19–20, 21–22, 72, 86
Arab Spring, 51, 62
arbitrage bots, 48, 93
Armenian Genocide, 11
ARPANET, 7, 155n2
artificial intelligence (AI)
   agent-based AI, 106–108
   AI winters, 105, 106
   bias, 146
   bot detection, 110–111
   bots and, 1–2, 97–119
   CAPTCHAs, 110–111
   chatbots
      AI assistants, 115–117, 146–147
      AI-based, 115, 150
      corpus-based, 114
      natural language processing, 112
      non-AI chatbots, 112–113
      open-domain, 118
   computing power, 104–105, 107
   conversational AI, 84–85, 115–117
   divergent behavior, 125

ethics, 145–150
fake AI, 101
fears, 139
funding, 105–106
future, 144
fuzzy logic, 114
history, 101, 102–103
meaning, 100–101
perceptron model, 102–103, 104
progress limits, 103–106
scholarship, 138, 149–152
scope, 99–100
social limits, 105
strong/general AI, 101
synthetic media, 142
terminology, 85, 102
time factor, 104
use by bots, 109–118
weak AI, 101
See also machine learning
Ashley Madison, 46
AskJeeves, 30
Assad, Bashar al-, 62–63
Assenmacher, D., 132
Associated Press, 44
astroturfing, 56, 57, 64–65
@AussieParlEdits, 75
Automated Retroactive Minimal Moderation (ARMM), 10
automated social actors (ASAs), 128–129
automatic speech recognition (ASR), 116, 117, 147
Autopolitic, 72
avatars, 90, 138
Avid Life Media, 46
Azerbaijan, 51, 56, 66

Bahrain, 51, 56, 63, 66
Bakardjieva, Maria, 36
banking, transactional bots, 88–89, 92–95
Bayesian methods, 115
Berners-Lee, Tim, 9, 86, 95, 106–107, 142–143

Biden, Joe, 1, 2
Bing, 2, 88
Bitcoins, 121
black hats, 78
black PR firms, 65
Blizzard, 47
Bloomberg, 47
Booch, G., 138–139
Borch, C., 94
bot ecology, 123, 131–132
Bot Sentinel, 110
botcheck.me, 110
Botivist, 76
Botnerds, 87
botnets, meaning, 27–28
bots
  characteristics, 29–30
    automation, 29
    coordination, 29
    intent, 29
    interaction, 29
    passivity, 29
    politicization, 30
    transparency, 29
  definition, 20, 28–30, 49
  diversity, 3–4
  etymology, 5–6
  functions, 4
  future, 140–152
  history. *See* history of bots
  routine maintenance, 2–3
  types. *See* types of bots
  See also specific bots
botwars, 17
Brexit, 67–68, 85
broadband, 18
Brown, Aaron, 94
Bucher, Taina, 122
bureaucrat bots, 24
Business Insider, 92, 96

Call of Duty, 47
Callon, Michel, 126–127
Cambridge Analytica, 72, 90
cancelbots, 10–11, 17
CancelBunny, 10

Index

Canter, Laurence, 16
Capek. Karel, 5
CAPTCHAs, 110–111
Carpenter, Rollo, 114
Castronova, Edward, 47
censorship, 11, 59, 60–62
Ceruzzi, Paul, 30, 100
chatbots
   AI assistants, 115–117, 146–147
   AI-based, 115, 150
   corpus-based, 114
   customer service, 3, 86, 91–92, 96, 112–113
   future, 141–142
   fuzzy logic, 114
   GPT chatbots, 118
   journalism, 42–43
   MUD, 13–14
   natural language processing and, 112
   non-AI chatbots, 112–113
   open-domain, 118
   origins, 6–8
   poitical use, 1
   social bots, 33, 37–40
   terminology, 85
   Turing test, 98
   typology, 23–24
chess matches, 101
China
   conversational AI assistants, 116
   political bots, 62, 63
   propaganda, 56
   surveillance, 73
   Tibet, 63
   trolling, 66
Chomsky, Noam, 60
Church of Scientology, 10
civil society, 76–77, 150
clear web, 16
Clearview AI, 73, 74
Cleverbot, 114
Clinton, Hilary, 67
clonebots, 13

Cloudfare, 64
CNN, 89
Cofacts, 76–77
cognitive behavioal therapy (CBT), 141–142
Colby, Kenneth, 142
collidebots, 13
Colombia, 51
commentary bots, 40
commercial bots
   crawlers, 87–88
   customer service, 3, 86, 91–92, 96, 112–113
   entertainmnent, 89–91
   finance, 88–89, 92–95
   informational bots, 89
   overview, 83–96
   spiders, 87–88
   transactional bots, 88–89, 92–95
   typology, 86–91
communicative bots, 123
@CongressEdits, 75
conversational AI assistants, 115–117
conversational user interfaces (CUIs), 141, 144, 146–147
Cooke, M., 39
coordinated inauthentic behavior (CIB), 56
Corbato, Fernando, 7
corruption, 76
Cortana, 3, 49, 85, 87, 107, 116
COVID-19, 1, 43
crawlers, 14–16, 17–18, 24–25, 87–88
Cruz, Ted, 72
cryptojacking, 28
CSS, 153n7
Cult of the Dead Cow (cDc), 10–11
customer service, 3, 86, 91–92, 96, 112–113
cyberattacks, 3, 26–27, 28
cybersecurity, 25, 26, 28, 78
cyborgs, 26, 78–79, 110, 111, 138

daemons, 6–8
Dalai Lama, 63
dampening, 59, 60–62, 63, 64
Dark Web, 121
data colonialism, 134
Data Skrive, 44
DataDome, 48
dating apps, 3, 46
deep fakes, 3, 82, 142, 148–149
deep learning (neural networks), 101, 103, 108, 109, 140, 146
deep web, 154n10
derivatives, 92
digital, etymology, 140
digital personal assistants, 37, 84, 86, 91
Discord, 89
distributed denial of services (DDoS) attacks, 26–27, 28, 63–64, 90
DoNotPay bot, 24, 95
DOTA 2, 48
Dourish, P., 125, 150
driverless cars, 101
drug trafficking, 121
Drupal, 39
dumb bots, 53, 57, 147
Dyn, 28

Ecuador, 56, 63–64, 66, 69
eggdrop bots, 12
EGHNA Development and Support, 63
ELIZA, 6–8, 13, 14, 22, 23, 37, 38, 39, 43, 76, 112, 113, 114, 147
email spam, 18, 84, 95
embodied interaction, 125
Emerj, 49
entertainmnent bots, 89–91
Erdogan, Recep Tayyip, 66
Estonia, 64
ethics, 145–150
etymology, 5–6, 140
European Union, 52

@everyword, 32–33, 35, 37, 40–41, 46
execution-oriented trade bots, 93

Facebook
  AI assistant, 47–48, 85
  bot technology, 49
  crawler bots, 17
  fake followers, 59
  fraudulent accounts, 142
  information gathering, 72, 73
  Messenger, 40
  political bots, 81
  scrapers, 90
  social bots, 41
  See also social media
farm bots, 48
feminism, 138
File Transfer Protocol (FTP), 9
finance, transactional bots, 88–89, 92–95
Finn, M., 45
fish, 153n6
Flash Crash (2010), 94
frame semantics, 117
fraud, 3, 48, 60, 90–91, 142, 157n2
future
  ethics, 145–149
  NLP, 141–142
  overview, 140–152
  policy issues, 144–145
  regulation of bots, 144–145
  scholarship, 149–152
  semantic web, 142–144
  synthetic media, 142
futures trading, 92
fuzzy logic, 114

GamerBot, 89
games, 3, 12, 13–14, 19, 46–48, 58, 82, 89–90, 101, 113
@GCCAedits, 75
Gehl, R.W., 36
Geiger, R.S., 92–93, 123, 135–136
gender, 138

generative adversarial networks (GANs), 111
generative pretrained transformer (GPT) chatbots, 118
Genies, 90
Geocities, 30
Georgia, 64
Gilmore, John, 61
Gingrich, Newt, 59
Girit, Selin, 66
Github, 57
Glassman, M., 47
Google
  AdLingo, 40
  bot technology, 49, 88
  CAPTCHA tests, 110
  Chrome, 22
  dominance, 15
  Google Assistant, 85
  Google Home, 23, 107, 116
  Jigsaw, 64
  Knowledge Graph, 116
  Meena bot, 118
  origin, 16
  Rich Business, 40
  use of bots, 2
Goostman (Eugene Goostman bot), 38, 39, 97–98, 99, 112
Gorwa, R., 20, 25, 26, 29
GOSU.AI, 48
GPT-3, 23–24, 82, 118, 142, 148
Gray, J., 48
Grey, Matthew, 15
Grimme, C., 132
Guglielmi, G., 1
Guilbeault, D., 20, 25, 26, 29, 123, 131–132
GUS, 117

Hacker News, 142, 148
hacking, 10–11, 12–13, 26–27, 63–64, 90
Hacking Team, 64
HAL 9000, 150

harassment, 51, 66, 69, 71, 148, 150
Haraway, D., 138
Harnad, Stephen, 38–39
hashtag poisoning, 61, 62–63
Hassard, J., 126–127
hate speech, 80, 83, 95, 125, 130
headless bots, 22
Hegelich, S., 129–130
Heliograf bot, 24
helper bots, 39, 86
Hepp, A., 123, 134
Herman, Edward, 60
high-frequency trading (HFT), 94
history of bots
  daemons, 6–8
  early internet, 8–11
  Internet Relay Chat (IRC), 11–13
  MUD environments, 13–14
  online gaming, 13–14
  overview, 6–14
  permanent development, 30
  proliferation, 11–13
  search engines, 14–16
  social bots, 18–20
  spambots, 16–18
  Usenet, 9–11
  web indexing, 14–16
  World Wide Web, 14–20
Howard, P.N., 34, 35, 130–131
human-bot relationship, 123, 128–133
human-computer interaction (HCI), 124–128, 150–151
human-machine communication, 124–128
Hwang, Tim, 132, 136–137
hypertext markup language (HTML), 15
hypertext transfer protocol (HTTP), 9

IBM, 7
impersonator bots, 90–91

indexing bots, 14–16, 25, 71
India, 56, 65, 69
@IndiaWatchBot, 43
information abundance, 61
informational bots, 89
infrastructural role of bots, 2, 8,
  12, 14, 19–20, 25, 34, 88,
  117, 133–137
Institute for the Future, 78
Internet of Things, 28, 143
Internet Relay Chat (IRC), 9,
  11–13, 14, 16, 17, 19, 23
Internet Research Agency (IRA),
  54–55, 59, 68
Italy, 79

Janetzko, D., 129–130
JavaScript, 153n7
Jeff_ebooks, 120–122, 124, 125,
  129, 145
@jeffrybooks, 120–122, 145
Jigsaw, 64
journalism, social bots and,
  41–45
Julia, 13–14

Kazemi, Darius, 40
Keller, M., 42
Kennedy, K., 131
Khashoggi, Jamal, 56
Kik, 85, 89
knowbots, 153n6
knowledge graphs, 116, 147
knowledge representation,
  116–117, 143
Ko Wen-je, 72
Koster, Martijn, 17, 154n9
Krebs, Brian, 63
Kushner, David, 41

Latour, Bruno, 39, 123, 126–127
Law, J, 126–127
League of Legends, 47, 48
Leck, Nigel, 76
Lee, Billion, 77
Lefkowitz, M., 103

Leonard, Andrew, 6, 10
Leonardo da Vinci, 5
Lewis-Kraus, G., 105
Liang, Johnson, 77
Lighthill Report, 105–106
LINE, 21
LinkedIn, 73
Lithuania, 64
Liveperson, 40
Loebner, Hugh, 98–99
Loebner Prize, 38, 99, 113
Long, K., 136
Los Angeles Times, 44
Luhn, Alec, 53
Lycos, 16

Maas-Neotek Family, 14
McCarthy, John, 102
machine learning
  bot detection, 110, 111
  chatbots, 23, 91
  development, 101, 107–108
  meaning, 103
  supervised, 108, 109
  terminology, 107–108
  unsupervised, 108–109
machine translation, 101, 103,
  105
Mackenzie, D., 92
Madella, Sadya, 84
malicious bots, 3, 11, 12–13, 18,
  25, 26–27, 41, 48, 63, 90,
  110, 134, 144–145, 150–151
malware, 90
Mandarin Chinese, 140
manufacturing consensus, 60,
  65–66, 123
Markov Chains, 11, 115, 120
Mashable, 46
Mastercard, 63
Mauldin, Michael, 14, 16, 153n1
@McYangin, 78
Mechanical Turk, 101
Meena bot, 118
megaphoning, 59, 64–66
mental health, 141–142

messaging app bots, 86
Messenger, 89
Mexico, 51, 62, 68–69, 79
Microsoft
 Bing, 2, 88
 bot technology, 49
 Clippy, 39
 Cortana, 3, 49, 85, 87, 107, 116
 Tay, 83–84, 85, 86, 87, 91, 95, 119, 125, 130, 136
 @zochats, 157n2
Miller, C., 131
Minebot, 47
Minecraft, 47, 90
Minsky, Marvin, 99, 103–104
Mirai botnet, 28
misogyny, 95
MockingJay, 42
Montfort, Nick, 32
Moore's law, 104
@mothgenerator, 37
Mozilla Firefox, 22
MUDbots, 13–14, 19, 23, 113
Mulaney, John, 110
Müller, P., 48
Myers, A., 101

Nadella, Satya, 84, 156n7
Nagy, P., 123, 130, 131
Namis, M., 132
Nardi, B., 123, 126, 128, 129
natural language processing (NLP), 11, 82, 109, 112, 113, 115, 141–142, 146–147
Neff, G., 123, 130, 131
Nemtsov, Boris, 51–55, 68
Netflix, 28
network theory, 123, 127
neural networks, 101, 103
neurons, 102
New Turkey Digital Office, 66
New York Times, 28, 42
news bots, 24
Nguyen, M.-H., 92
Nigeria, 70
Noble, S., 36, 138

North Macedonia, 70
@NYPDedits, 41–42, 71

Oikarinen, Jarkko, 12
OkCupid, 46
open-source intelligence (OSINT), 73–74
OpenAI, 23–24
Operation Payback, 63
optical character recognition (OCR), 110
O'Reilly, 84–85, 156n7
Overwolf, 48
OVH, 28
Oxford Internet Institute (OII), 67

pandemic, 1, 43
paranoid schizophrenia, 98
Park, A., 93–94
Park Geun-Hye, 69–70
Parks, M.R., 34, 35
@Parliamentedits, 75
Parrish, Allison, 32, 33, 35–36, 37
PARRY, 98
Patch, 44
pattern matching, 7, 76, 112, 113, 114, 115
Paypal, 63
Pearce, L., 132
Peiser, J., 44
Peña Nieto, Enrique, 68–69
perceptron, 102–103, 104
pervasive conversational user interfaces (CUIs), 141
PhantomJS, 22
Philippines, 56, 66, 69
Pinkerton, Brian, 16
Plaisant, C., 125
Polish, 29
political bots
 ABC model, 57
 algorithms, 58–59
 amplification, 59, 64–66, 67, 76

Index

analytics, 71–74
arms race, 77–81, 110
censorship, 60–62
characteristics, 30
cyborgs, 26
dampening, 59, 60–62
DDoS attacks, 26–27, 28, 63–64
harassment, 66
hashtag poisoning, 61, 62–63
identifying, 57
influencing voter turnout, 70
information gathering, 71–74
manufacturing consensus, 60
megaphoning, 59, 64–66
misuse, 150
overview, 51–82
public attitude to, 85
reputation management, 65
Russia, 51–56
social activism, 75–77
social media, 40
spambots, 25
surveillance, 70–75
  active, 74–75
  passive, 71–74
tactics, 58–66
transparency bots, 74–75
uses, 67–77
Preece, J., 124–125
privacy rights, 42, 73, 74, 80
probability techniques, 115
Project Shield, 64
propaganda, connotations, 155n14
proxies, 46, 123, 131, 137
psychotherapy, 142
PUDG model, 33, 35
Punzalan, R., 123, 134–135
Puppeteer, 22
Putin, Vladimir, 52
Python, 154n12

QSearch, 72
Quakebot, 44
Quartz, 43, 156n5

racism, 83–84, 95
Random Darknet Shopper, 121, 124, 129
Reading University, 98
Reddit, 3, 13, 21, 35, 36–37, 39, 135, 136
religions, 65, 148
reputation management, 65
reverse engineering, 58–59
@RiksdagWikiEdit, 75
Robertson, J., 54
Robot Exclusion Standard (RES), 17–18
robots, etymology, 5
Rosenblatt, Frank, 102, 103
RoverBot, 17–18, 25
Royal Society, 38, 98
Russia
  annexation of Crimea, 52
  DDoS attacks, 64
  hacking, 60
  political bots, 51–56, 62, 68
  pro-democracy activism, 77
  trolling, 66
  volunteer botnets, 79

Samsung, 65
Saudi Arabia, 56
Savchuk, Lyudmila, 54
scams, 3, 25, 41, 101, 157n2
Schneiderman, B., 125
Schreckinger, B., 81
scrapers, 22, 86, 90
search engines, 14–16, 25, 30, 58, 88
Searle, John, 101
Second Life, 19, 47
Secondlife, 48
Sedar Argic, 11
Selemium, 22
self-driving cars, 145
semantic web, 86, 106–107, 142–144, 146–147
service bots, 24
Shah, Huma, 38
Shaney, Mark V., 11

Shorey, S., 130–131
Simon, Herbert, 103
simulation trading bots, 93
Singh, Rampal, 65
Siri, 2, 23, 49, 85, 87, 107, 116
situated action, 123, 126
Slack, 89
smartphones, 6, 49
social bots
  agency, 132–133
  amplification techniques, 23
  APIs, 21–22
  behavioral theory, 129–130
  characteristics, 33, 34, 37–41
  chatbots, 37–40
  commerce, 86
  cyborgs, 26
  future, 144–145
  global society, 34–37
  human-bot relationship, 130
  identifying, 40–41
  informational bots, 89
  journalism and, 41–45
  meaning, 22–23
  origin, 18–20
  overview, 32–50
  proliferation, 21
  proxies, 131
  shortcomings, 132
  social media and, 39–40
social media
  agency, 131–133
  algorithms, 58
  astroturfing, 56
  bots, 1–3
  commentary bots, 40
  commercial objectives, 96
  dawn of social bots, 18–20
  fake accounts, 56
  hashtag poisoning, 62–63
  identity, 122–123
  impersonator bots, 90–91
  information gathering, 71–74
  political bots, 40
  social bots and, 39–40
  spambots, 25

transparency, 80
transparency bots, 74–75
See also specific media
sock puppets, 29
South Korea, 69–70
Soviet Union, 126
S&P 500 index, 94
spam, 18, 84, 95
spambots, 16–18, 25, 86, 90, 157n2
spiders, 14–16, 24–25, 87–88
Sportradar, 44
statistics, etymology, 140
Steiner, David, 41
stock markets, 3, 94
Suchman, L., 123, 125, 129
Summers, E., 123
surveillance, 70–75, 134, 147
Switzerland, 121
synthetic media, 142, 148–149
Syria, 51, 62–63

Taiwan, 24–25, 59, 65, 68, 72, 76–77
Tay, 83–84, 85, 86, 87, 91, 95, 119, 125, 130, 136
@TayandYou, 83–84
Telegram, 21, 49, 148–149
Terminator, 150
theory
  human-bot relationship, 128–133
  human-computer interaction, 124–128
  infrastructural role of bots, 133–137
  overview, 120–139
  research directions, 137–139
Tinder, 46, 79
TinyMUD environments, 14
trading bots, 86, 92–94, 96
transactional bots, 88–89, 92–95
translation, 101, 103, 105
transparency, 29, 71, 74–75, 80–81, 144–145, 145, 150, 151

Triquet, François, 156n6
trolls
  identifying, 2, 150
  meaning, 28–29
  politics, 25, 66
  practice, 55–56, 66, 69
  Russia, 53, 54
  Tay, 95, 130
Trump, Donald, 1, 67, 72
Tufekci, Z., 61
Turing, Alan, 37–38, 97
Turing test, 38, 97–99, 110, 129
Turkey, 11, 51, 66
Twitter
  API, 19–20, 21, 166n1
  astroturfing, 65
  bot detection, 110
  Bot Sentinel, 110
  botcheck.me, 110
  bots and, 19–20
  @congressgunbot, 71
  cyberattacks, 28
  cyborgs, 78
  death threats, 120
  Dictator Alert, 75
  @everyword, 32–33, 35, 37, 40–41, 46
  fake followers, 59
  fraudulent accounts, 142
  hashtag poisoning, 62
  @IndiaWatchBot, 43
  @jeffrybooks, 120–122, 145
  @McYangin, 78
  @mothgenerator, 37
  @NYPDedits, 40
  political bots, 53–55, 57, 67–70
  public space, 33
  social activism, 76
  social bots, 39, 42
  spam, 81, 90
  Tay. *See* Tay
  transparency bots, 75
  trolling, 66
  @Twoheadlines, 40–41
  See also social media
@Twoheadlines, 40–41

types of bots
  APIs, 21–22
  botnets, 27–28
  bureaucrat bots, 24
  chatbots, 23–24
  crawlers/spiders, 24–25
  cyborgs, 26
  overview, 20–28
  service bots, 24
  social bots, 22–23
  spambots, 25
  zombies, 26–27
  See also specific types

Ukraine, 52, 64, 77
United Kingdom
  Brexit referendum, 67–68, 85
  cyborgs, 79
  Lighthill Report, 105–106
United States
  2016 presidential election, 2, 49, 59, 67–68, 72, 85, 90
  2018 mid-term elections, 157n2
  2020 presidential election, 1–2
  ALPAC Report, 105–106
  automated financial trading, 94
  Capitol storming (6 January 2021), 1
  net neutrality, 60
  regulation of bots, 144
  sanctions against Russia, 52
  War on Terror, 75
Unix, 9
Usenet, 9–11, 12, 14, 16–17, 19, 23, 115

van der Goot, Jeffry, 120–122, 129, 145
Veale, T., 39
Venezuela, 56, 62, 66, 77
Venmo, 42, 73
VentureBeat, 48
video games, 3, 46–48, 82, 89–90
Visa, 63

Index

volunteer botnets, 26, 78–79
votebots, 22, 24–25

walkers, 153n6
wanderers, 15, 153n6
Wang, J., 93–94
Warnick, Kevin, 38
Washington Post, 24, 42–43
web robots, 153n6
WebCrawler, 16
Weizenbaum, Joseph, 7–8, 23, 38, 142
WhatsApp, 40, 49, 89
white hats, 78, 80
Wikileaks, 63
Wikipedia
  bots, 3, 123
  edits, 40, 41–42, 74–75
  infrastructure bots, 135–136
  @NYPDedits, 40, 41–42
  social bots, 39, 42
  transactional bots, 92–93
Winner, L., 124, 127–128, 150
Woebot, 141
Won Sei-hoon, 69–70
Woolley, Samuel, 123, 130–131, 133, 136–137, 138
WordPress, 39
World of Warcraft, 47

World Wide Web
  advertising, 19
  development of bots, 14–20
  origin, 9
  semantic web, 86, 106–107, 142–144, 146–147
  spambots, 16–18
  web-indexing bots, 14–16, 25, 71
World Wide Web Wanderer, 15
Writergate, 65
Wxcafe, 121
Wyse, 141

@XiaoIce, 40–41, 85, 86, 91

Yandex, 2
Yang, Andrew, 26, 78
YangGang RT bot, 26
Yeltsin, Boris, 52
Youper, 141
@YourRepsOnGuns, 71
YouTube, 3, 21, 44, 58, 73

Zhenhua Data, 73, 74
@zochats, 157n2
zombies, 26–27
Zuboff, S., 134
Zuckerberg, Mark, 81, 84